The Little Capoeira Book

Nestor Capoeira

translated by
Alex Ladd

North Atlantic Books
Berkeley, California

The Little Capoeira Book

Published by
North Atlantic Books
P.O. Box 12327
Berkeley, CA 94712

Cover art by Edson Campos
Artwork of movements, sequences and kicks by Silas Queiroz
Back-cover photograph by Zé Roberto (from the film *Cordão de Ouro* by A.C. Fontura)
Black-and-white photographs provided by Dr. Maurício Vinhas de Queiroz (These photographs were taken in the 1950s, and depict the *roda* of Mestre Valdemar da Paixão (striped shirt), one of the great *Angoleiros* of his time.
Drawing of Mestre Bimba by Bodinho, from the *Jornal da Capoeira*
Cover and book design by Paula Morrison
Printed in the United States of America

The Little Capoeira Book is sponsored by the Society for the Study of Native Arts and Sciences, a nonprofit educational corporation whose goals are to develop an educational and crosscultural perspective linking various scientific, social, and artistic fields; to nurture a holistic view of the arts, sciences, humanities, and healing; and to publish and distribute literature on the relationship of mind, body, and nature.

Library of Congress Cataloging-in-Publication Data

Capoeira, Nestor
[Pequeno manual do jogador de capoeira. English]
The little capoeira book / Nestor Capoeira : translated by Alex Ladd.
    p. cm.
   ISBN 1-55643-199-6
   1. Capoeira (Dance)   I. Title.
GV1796.C145C3513   1995
793.33—dc20   95-2216
                                            CIP

1 2 3 4 5 6 7 8 9 / 99 98 97 96 95

NESTOR CAPOEIRA

This book is dedicated to Dermeval Lopez de Lacerda, Mestre Leopoldina, who introduced me to the mysteries and the *malandragens* of capoeira; and to all of the players past, present and future.

TABLE OF CONTENTS

Preface by the Translator ix

Preface xiii

History 1

    Introduction 3

    Origins 3

    During Slavery 5

    The Freeing of the Slaves 10

    Bimba and Pastinha 13

    The Recent Years 15

    Capoeira in the 1970s and 1980s 17

    Capoeira Nowadays — the 1990s 19

O Jogo **(The game)** 21

    Yê Vamos Embora, Camará! 23

    The *Roda* (The Circle) 24

    A Game, a Fight or a Dance? 29

    The Three Levels of the Game 30

    Malícia 33

    The Origins of *Malícia:* The Slave and the Bandit 34

The Music 39

    Music and Capoeira 41

    The *Berimbau* 41

    The Chants 45

Learning Capoeira 53

    Presentation of Movements 60

Defensive Movements 71

The Basic Kicks 73

Bimba's Sequences 86

Takedowns 108

Other Kicks and Movements 124

The Language of Angola 135

Final Words 139

Final Words to the English Edition 141

Glossary of Basic Capoeira Terms 143

A PREFACE BY THE TRANSLATOR

I remember seeing a capoeira exhibition for the first time as a small boy in a hotel in Salvador, Bahia—Brazil's undisputed capital of Afro-Brazilian culture. Two sinewy, bare-chested men took the hotel's stage and proceeded to awe that child with moves that until then I had thought were restricted to comic-book heroes—and all of this done to the infectious beat of exotic instruments with names like *berimbau, reco-reco, pandeiro, atabaque* and *agô-gô*.

As a college student, twelve years later, seeking to enroll in a martial arts class, I thought again about the exhibition that I had seen in Bahia. Why not study a martial art whose roots in this hemisphere were so deep and rich? But could it be that this unique art form was being taught in the United States?

To my surprise, I found that not only was capoeira being taught but that a burgeoning capoeira "scene" was developing in this country under the vigilant eyes of some pioneering Brazilian masters.

Among the first to come to the States and teach regularly, around 1974, were two young natives of Salvador with impressive capoeira credentials, Mestre (Master) Jelon Vieira and Loremil Machado (1953–1994).[1] Machado eventually gravitated towards performance and dance, while Vieira embarked on the difficult path of molding American capoeiristas on a par with their Brazilian counterparts.

A typical Vieira class in New York city during the '70s and '80s might include a Yale hockey player who could easily relate to this

---

1. Mestre Vieira was a pupil of Mestre Bôbô, Mestre Bimba and Mestre Eziquiel, and Machado studied with Mestre Nô.

THE LITTLE CAPOEIRA BOOK

mix of grace and muscle; an African-American jazz musician who found capoeira's African-structured songs a throwback to his own roots; and a classical ballet dancer mesmerized by capoeira's beautiful yet lethal movements. All seemed to find something in this unique art form.

In 1978, Mestre Acordeon (Bira Almeida), one of legendary Mestre Bimba's (1900–1974) leading pupils, arrived in California and began sharing his rich capoeira vision with his students there. He has been teaching consistently in the San Francisco Bay Area[2] ever since. His book, *Capoeira: A Brazilian Art Form* (North Atlantic Books, 1986) was one of the first published on the subject matter in this country and is still one of the best sources available for those wishing to learn the history and philosophy of this art form.

Soon there were many others, including the venerable Angoleiro Mestre João Grande, a former student of Mestre Pastinha (1890–1981), the foremost practitioner of the traditional *capoeira Angola* style of his generation. Mestre João Grande came to the United States in 1990, undaunted by his age and the cultural and language barriers he would face, and armed with the faith that he would communicate in the universal language of capoeira—and he was right. With the opening of his *academia* in New York City, where he continues to teach, he became one of the first capoeira mestres to have a school in the U.S. dedicated solely to the teaching of capoeira.

Add to those names Brazil's first woman mestre, Edna Lima (who also teaches in New York), plus several talented young Brazilian and American mestres and professors teaching all over the United States, from Boston to Santa Fé, who have all contributed in their own way, and all of a sudden we have a capoeira "scene."[3]

---

2. Today there are over a dozen people teaching capoeira in the Bay Area alone.

3. The list of Mestres I have mentioned here is by no means complete. Many other talented mestres and teachers whom I have not mentioned for lack of space have contributed and are contributing to the growth of capoeira

For all of this activity, however, capoeira remains a foreign word to most Americans, not unlike many of the Asian martial arts in this country in the early 1950s. Although Nestor Capoeira resides in Brazil, perhaps the publication of his *Little Capoeira Book* in English will be one more step in giving capoeira the recognition it is due.

With this book we have for the first time in this country a manual that breaks down basic capoeira moves, with the help of easy-to-understand diagrams combined with insights into the history, ritual and philosophy of the game. Anyone who has studied martial arts knows that it is impossible to learn from a book alone—you must also "do." This is even more true of capoeira, which is so much more than a martial art and which demands participation on many levels. Nonetheless, this book can serve as an excellent introduction, guide and reference for both the beginner and the more advanced student.

Part athlete, part bohemian philosopher and part scholar, Nestor Capoeira embodies traits that make him singularly qualified to write on the subject matter. Nestor, as he likes to be called, is a former student of the legendary Mestre Leopoldina (who in turn was a pupil of Quinzinho and Mestre Arthur Emidío). Later he joined the Senzala group where he studied under Mestre Preguiça (Vandencolque de Oliveira).[4] In 1969, he obtained that group's coveted red-cord and later became one of *Senzala's* leading members.

Nestor Capoeira combines the knowledge of one who has done (and is doing) with that of a serious scholar and chronicler of the art. He is a frequent figure at conferences on this art form, and has been the official chronicler of several national and international capoeira encounters. He has taught capoeira non-stop since 1969, has three books published on the subject, and was a pioneer in

---

in this country—people like Preguiça, Marcelo and Deraldo, to name a few. For a more complete chronology of the early years of capoeira in this country, read Bira Almeida's book, which was previously mentioned.

4. Mestre Preguiça has been teaching in the Bay Area since 1984.

introducing capoeira to Europe, where he first taught in 1971. Through Nestor's eyes we can get a sense of the historical perspective of capoeira as well as recent trends.

Hopefully, this book will help to inspire a new generation of capoeiristas in this country. For those who doubt that this art form can be transplanted to American soil, it is necessary only to see top American capoeiristas in action. They have internalized the capoeira vocabulary and philosophy, and have achieved the ultimate compliment when Brazilian capoeiristas mistake them for one of their own. Their mastery is achieved through incredible hard work and dedication. I hope that this book will play a part in helping to spawn more capoeiristas like them.

—Alex Ladd (a.k.a. Graveto)

Alex Ladd was born in Rio de Janeiro, Brazil in 1964. He began studying capoeira in 1986 with Mestre Jelon Vieira and later studied with Mestra Edna Lima. He currently resides in New Jersey, where he works as a free-lance writer and translator.

PREFACE

In 1971, while I was teaching capoeira at the London School of Contemporary Dance, I wrote a little manual and photocopied it for my students. I felt they needed some information on the history and philosophy of capoeira in order to understand what the *jogo* (game) they were learning in my classes was all about.

Those pages were the beginning of something that has grown in the last twenty-five years, which today is part of my relationship with capoeira and the capoeira world: I have since published three books on the subject in Brazil and now I am happy to see my first book translated into English and published in the United States.

Of course, during all of this time a lot of new research and information has been brought out, and many of my insights on the history of capoeira have changed. I have also grown a bit older and more experienced in the game—of life and of capoeira—and have had the chance to strengthen my links with players and *mestres* older than myself, capoeiristas I had admired when young and whom I now call my friends. These friendships brought with them a richness of information—philosophical knowledge of the roots and the ritual of the game—as well as shared experiences which spanned many years. This, of course, deepened my understanding of what capoeira is all about. I am happy to say that this new material is present in this first English edition, and I hope it can transmit this information that has enriched my vision of capoeira.

So my purpose in this "little book" is twofold:

1) to inform the reader about capoeira, its history, philosophy, music, ritual, myth and significance; and

2) to provide a practical method of teaching and learning that will properly introduce the beginner from a different culture to the capoeira game.

Capoeira has enriched my life, has opened many doors and given me unexpected opportunities in these last thirty years. I have observed that I am not the only one who has benefited from it, and I hope that the reader will shortly join our *roda* (circle).

—Nestor Capoeira

THE HISTORY

Camará, donde é que vens, camará;
camará, donde é que vens, camará?

Comrade, from whence do you come, comrade;
comrade, from whence do you come, comrade?

INTRODUCTION

In 1500 the Portuguese, led by explorer Pedro Alves Cabral, arrived in Brazil.

One of the first measures taken by the new arrivals was the subjugation of the local population—the Brazilian Indians—in order to furnish the Portuguese with slave labor.

The experience with the aborigines was a failure—the Indians quickly died in captivity or fled to their nearby homes. The Portuguese then began to import slave labor from Africa. On the other side of the Atlantic, free men and women were captured, loaded onto ghastly slave ships and sent on a nightmarish voyage that for most would end in perpetual bondage.

The Africans first arrived by the hundreds and later by the thousands. They brought with them their culture—vibrant and different from the European one—a culture that was not stored away in books or museums but rather in the body, mind, heart and soul; a culture that was transmitted from father to son, from the initiate to the novice throughout the generations.

There was *candomblé,* a religion; the *berimbau,* a musical instrument; *vatapá,* a food; and so many other things—in short, a way of life. This book makes reference to a small part of that vast whole—the game of capoeira.

ORIGINS

The origins of capoeira—whether African or Brazilian—are cause for controversy to this day; different and opposing theories have been created to explain how it all began. Unfortunately, the early days of capoeira are shrouded in mystery, since few documents exist from that era regarding capoeira, and research on the matter is still in its initial stages.

But so that we may better understand the subject, let us also embark on a terrible voyage similar to that of the slave ships as they carried their human cargo to a life of slavery.

Let us imagine the landing of a flying saucer arriving from a distant planet. Its crew members carry terrible and unknown weapons. A great number of people, among general chaos and bloodshed, are captured.

After the frightful voyage, we arrive at our new home. There we are sold into slavery, and after the first days of arduous work we are taken to rest in the common slave quarters. We get to know our companions in this calamity: an American guitar player, an English boxer, a Brazilian samba percussionist, a Chinese tai-chi practitioner, and an African *swat* player—among many others.

Time goes by, and during the rare moments of leisure we begin to absorb each other's culture. Our children, and the children of our children, are born and raised in this environment of heterogeneous cultures and enslavement. Let us imagine that gradually, over several decades, a new form of cultural expression is born—a dance-fight, a game that is a mixture of boxing, tai-chi, samba, American music and the *swat*.

Now we have an idea of how capoeira was born and what its origins were: a synthesis of dances, fights and musical instruments from different cultures, from different African regions. It is a synthesis created on Brazilian soil, probably in Salvador, the capital of the state of Bahia, under the regime of slavery primarily during the nineteenth century.[5]

---

5. Capoeira developed in other parts of Brazil also, particularly in Rio de Janeiro and in Recife, where strong capoeira traditions could be found in the nineteenth century. In those cities capoeira maintained only its original fighting aspect and did not develop the synthesis between ritual and fight found in Bahia. Later, in the beginning of the twentieth century, the capoeira traditions in these two cities were extinguished by the police.

Condemned to a whipping in the public square. Debret, 1834

DURING SLAVERY

Starting around 1814, capoeira and other forms of African cultural expression suffered repression and were prohibited in some places by the slave masters and overseers.

Up until that date, forms of African cultural expression were permitted and sometimes even encouraged, not only as a safety gauge against the internal pressures created by slavery but also to bring out the differences between various African groups, in a spirit of "divide and conquer."

But with the arrival in Brazil in 1808 of the Portuguese king Dom João VI and his court, who were fleeing Napoleon Bonaparte's invasion of Portugal, things changed: The newcomers understood the necessity of destroying a people's culture in order to

Jogar capoeira *or* danse de la guerre *(Rugendas, 1824)*

dominate them, and capoeira began to be persecuted in a process which would culminate with its being outlawed in 1892.

Why was capoeira suppressed? The motives were many:

- It gave the Africans a sense of nationality.
- It developed self-confidence in individual capoeira practitioners.
- It created small, cohesive groups.
- It created dangerous and agile fighters.
- Sometimes the slaves would injure themselves during the capoeira game, which was not desirable from an economic point of view.

The masters and the overseers were probably not as conscious as the king and the intellectuals of his court of all of these motives, but intuitively—by that intuition which is inherent in any dominant class—they knew that something did not "smell right."

How was capoeira practiced, then?

- In a violent form in Rio de Janeiro and Recife.
- As a ritual-dance-fight-game in Bahia, where capoeira progressively absorbed other African elements.
- Sometimes in hiding, and in other places openly, in defiance of laws designed to abolish it.

Capoeira at that time had little in common with the capoeira that is practiced today or during the last one hundred years.

Take, for example, a description by the German artist Rugendas. His drawings of what he called *"Capüera, danse de la guerre"* ("Capoeira, war dance") and his written description of what he witnessed (*Voyage Picturesque et Historique dans le Bresil*, Engelman & Co., Paris 1824) are some of the first records we have of capoeira:[6]

> The Negroes have yet another war-like past-time, which is much more violent—capoeira: two champions throw themselves at each other, trying to strike their heads at the chest of the adversary whom they are trying to knock over. The attack is avoided with leaps to the sides and with stationary maneuvers which are equally as skillful, but in launching themselves at each other it so happens that they strike their heads together with great force, and it is not rare that the game degenerates into a fight, causing knifes to be brought into the picture, and bloodying the sport.

Absent from Rugendas' description are the acrobatic jumps, the ground movements, the leg blows, and the musical instrument called the *berimbau,* which had not yet been incorporated into the

---

6. Confirming this version of a more violent early capoeira, we have a letter from 1821, from the Military Commission of Rio de Janeiro to the War Ministry, complaining of "capoeira Negroes arrested by the military school for disorderly conduct." The letter recommends public punishment as a deterrent, and states that "there have been six deaths attributed to the before-mentioned capoeiras as well as several knife injuries."

game of capoeira. The *berimbau* is a one-stringed instrument with a gourd attached; its simplicity belies the range of sound an experienced player can summon from it. Ironically, today it is often considered indispensable and indeed dictates the rhythm and nature of the game—slower or faster, more combative or playful, treacherous or harmonious, etc.

In those days, capoeira was accompanied only by the *atabaque* (similar to the conga drum), hand-clapping and singing, as shown in Rugendas' drawing.

As time went by, this early capoeira described by Rugendas evolved and changed, partly through the mere passage of time—everything changes with time—and partly through the influence of other forms of fighting and dance coming from Africa, such as this dance described in a passage by Curt Sachs in *World History of Dance:*

> Two dancers and a singer take their places in the center of the circle. One sings praises to the old chiefs and maybe also to his favorite bull, and marks the rhythm with hand claps, while the other two dancers execute acrobatic moves and flips.

Musicians and acrobat during an African burial in Brazil (Debret 1834).

It must be stressed that there are many other theories attempting to explain the origins of capoeira.

According to one prevalent theory, capoeira was a fight that was disguised as a dance so that it could be practiced unbeknownst to the white slave owners. This seems unlikely because, around 1814, when African culture began to be repressed, other forms of African dancing suffered prohibition along with capoeira, so there was no sense in disguising capoeira as a dance.

Another theory says that the Mucupes in the South of Angola had an initiation ritual (*efundula*) for when girls became women, on which occasion the young warriors engaged in the *N'golo,* or "dance of the zebras," a warrior's fight-dance. According to this theory, the N'golo was capoeira itself. This theory was presented by Câmara Cascudo (*Folclore do Brasil,* 1967), but one year later Waldeloir Rego (*Capoeira Angola,* Editora Itapoan, Salvador, 1968) warned that this "strange theory" should be looked upon with reserve until it was properly proven (something that never happened). If the *N'Golo* did exist, it would seem that it was at best one of several dances that contributed to the creation of early capoeira.

Other theories mix Zumbi, the legendary leader of the Quilombo dos Palmares (a community made up of those who managed to flee from slavery) with the origins of capoeira, without any reliable information on the matter.

All of these theories are extremely important when we try to understand the myth that surrounds capoeira, but they clearly cannot be accepted as historical fact according to the data and information that we presently have. Perhaps with further research the theory that we have proposed here, i.e., capoeira as a mix of various African dances and fights that occurred in Brazil, primarily in the 19th century, will also be outdated in future years.[7]

---

7. We say that the mixture of the capoeira described by Rugendas (1824) with other African elements happened in the nineteenth century, but when this original capoeira began to be practiced we do not know.

THE FREEING OF THE SLAVES

With the signing of the Golden Law in 1888, which abolished slavery, the newly freed blacks did not find a place for themselves within the existing socio-economic order. The capoeirista, with his fighting skills, self-confidence, and individuality, quickly descended into criminality—and capoeira along with him.

In Rio de Janeiro, where capoeira had developed exclusively as a form of fighting, criminal gangs were created that terrorized the population. Soon thereafter, during the transition from the Brazilian Empire to the Brazilian Republic in 1890, these gangs were used by both monarchists and republicans to exert pressure on and break up the rallies of their adversaries. The club, the dagger and the switchblade were used to complement the damage done by such capoeira moves as the *rabo de arraia* and the *rasteira.*

In Bahia, on the other hand, capoeira continued to develop into a ritual-dance-fight-game, and the *berimbau* began to be an indispensable instrument used to command the *rodas,* which always

A capoeirista delivers a deadly blow with his razorblade (Kalixto, 1906).

took place in hidden locales since the practice of capoeira in this era had already been outlawed by the first constitution of the Brazilian Republic (1892).

We now arrive at the year 1900.

In Rio, the capoeirista was a *malandro* (a rogue) and a criminal—whether he be white, mulatto or black—expert in the use of kicks (*golpes*), sweeps (*rasteiras*) and head-butts (*cabeçadas*), as well as in the use of blade weapons. In Recife, capoeira became associated with the city's principal music bands. During carnival time, tough capoeira fighters would lead the bands through the streets of that city, and wherever two bands would meet, fighting and bloodshed would usually ensue.

In turn-of-the-century Bahia, the capoeira[8] was also often seen as a criminal. But the players and the game exhibited all of the traits that still characterize it to this day.

The persecution and the confrontations with the police continued. The art form was slowly extinguished in Rio and Recife, leaving capoeira only in Bahia. It was during this period that legendary figures—feared players, *de corpo fechado*[9] such as Besouro Cordão-de-Ouro in Bahia, Nascimento Grande in Recife and Manduca da Praia in Rio, who are celebrated to this day in capoeira verses—made their appearances.

It is said that Besouro lived in Santo Amaro da Purificação in the State of Bahia, and that he was the teacher of another famous capoeirista by the name of Cobrinha Verde, whom I met in Bahia in the 1960s. Besouro did not like the police and was feared not only as a capoeira player but as an expert in the use of blade weapons, and also for having his *corpo fechado*. According to legend, an ambush was set up for him. It is said that he himself (who could not read)

---

8. *Capoeira* can be used to denote the art form or, as in this case, the practitioner of the art form (who can also be called a *capoeirista*).

9. *Corpo fechado* (closed body): A person who, through specific magic rituals, supposedly attains almost complete invulnerability in the face of various weapons.

carried the written message identifying him as the person to be killed, thinking that it was a message that would bring him work. Legend says he was killed with a special wooden dagger prepared during magic rituals in order to overcome his *corpo fechado.*

Of all the rogues who led the carnival bands through the streets of Recife, Nascimento Grande was one of the most feared. Some say that he was killed during the police persecution in the early 1900s, but others say he moved from Recife to Rio de Janeiro and died there of old age.

Manduca da Praia was of an earlier generation (1890s) and always dressed in an extremely elegant style. It is said that he owned a fish store and lived comfortably. He was also one of those who controlled elections in the area he lived in. He was said to have twenty-seven criminal cases against him (for assault, knifing, etc.) but was always absolved due to the influence of the politicians he worked for.

Later on, in the 1930s in Salvador, Mestre Bimba (Manuel dos Reis Machado—1900–1974) opened the first capoeira academy (1932), a feat made possible by the nationalistic policies of Getulio Vargas, who wanted to promote capoeira as a Brazilian sport.[10] From that moment on, Bimba began to teach capoeira in his *Centro de Cultura Física Regional Baiano.* In 1941, Mestre Pastinha (Vicente Ferreira Pastinha—1889–1981) opened his *capoeira Angola* school. For the first time, capoeira began to be taught and practiced openly in a formal setting.

---

10. Although Bimba opened his school in 1932, the official recognition only came about in 1937, when it was technically registered. It must be noted that the Getulio Vargas government permitted the practice of capoeira, but only in enclosed areas that were registered with the police. Vargas believed that physical education could be used to instill a sense of discipline in children if taught at an early age. He thought that capoeira, if transformed into a "sport," could help. In fact, much later, in 1955, he personally congratulated Mestre Bimba for turning capoeira into Brazil's "national fight."

BIMBA AND PASTINHA

The two central figures in capoeira in the twentieth century were undoubtedly Mestre Bimba and Mestre Pastinha. In fact, these two figures are so important in the history of capoeira that they (and the legend that surrounds them) are the mythical ancestors of all capoeira players, and much of what we are or try to be is due to what these men were or represented.

Mestre Bimba was born Manoel dos Reis Machado in 1900. He was initiated in capoeira when he was twelve years old, in an area known today as Liberdade, in Salvador. His mestre was the African Bentinho, a captain of a maritime company in Bahia. Bimba opened a school at the age of eighteen, but it was only in the 1930s that he opened his first academy, where he started teaching what he called "the regional fight from Bahia," eventually known as *Capoeira Regional.*

Bimba was a feared fighter who earned the nick-name "Três Pancadas" (or Three Hits) which, it was said, were the maximum number of blows that his adversaries could take from him. Nonetheless, Bimba espoused the *malandro* philosophy of "brain over brawn." He was fond of saying, *"Quem aguenta tempestade é rochedo,"* ("Only cliffs face the tempest"), which meant that if you are faced by someone much stronger than you, the smart thing to do is to run; but if he were to run after you, then you could get him unexpectedly—a typical *malandro* attitude.

With the opening of Bimba's academy, a new era in the history of capoeira began, as the game was taught to the children of the upper classes of Salvador.

Bimba introduced sweeps from *batuque,* a form of fighting in which

Mestre Bimba in his thirties

his father was proficient, and new *golpes ligados,* or connected blows. He also created a new teaching method based on eight sequences of predetermined moves and kicks for two players, and on the *cintura desprezada*—sequences of flips in which the capoeirista learns to always fall on his feet (see page 86). He essentially sacrificed much of the ritual and "game" aspects, as well as the slower rhythms, in favor of greater aggressiveness and fighting spirit.

All of this, added to the very important fact that the majority of his students belonged to another social class (meaning in turn that they possessed different backgrounds and values, and a different way of thinking than the traditional capoeirista, who belonged to the underprivileged classes deeply rooted in Afro-Brazilian culture), contributed to the creation of a new style known as *Capoeira Regional.*

In the years following the opening of his academy, Bimba had great success. He and his pupils performed in São Paulo, Rio de Janeiro and other major cities of Brazil. But in the beginning of the 1970s, dissatisfied with the official institutions of Bahia that had never helped him, he decided to move to Goiana (near Brasilia, the capital of Brazil). One year later, on February 5, 1974, he died in that city. Up until the last day of his life, he was active and extremely lucid. As a matter of fact, he planned to give an exhibition in a club that same afternoon. Although he had asked to be buried in Goiana, some of his former pupils got together and brought his body back to Salvador, where he had taught and practiced capoeira all of his life.

Many other individuals created and began to teach new forms of capoeira, but they did not possess Bimba's breadth of knowledge nor his personality, and these novelties disappeared just as quickly as they appeared.

With the advent of the *Regional* style, the traditional capoeira style became known as *Capoeira Angola.* During the time when the *Regional* and *Senzala* styles eclipsed *Capoeira Angola,* Pastinha and his group were practically the only ones that still preserved the traditional style, although some other groups were still active.

Vicente Ferreira Pastinha, Mestre Pastinha, was born in 1889.

He is said to have learned capoeira from an African from Angola named Benedito, who took the young Pastinha under his wing after witnessing him being repeatedly beaten up by an older boy. In spite of his small stature, at the age of sixteen Pastinha became a sort of a bouncer for a gambling house in a tough part of town. He opened his first academy a few years after Bimba's opened and, due to his charisma and leadership as well as his friendly way of dealing with others, he was able to attract a devoted group of pupils and capoeiristas that made his academy famous as a gathering point for artists and intellectuals who wanted to see the traditional *Capoeira Angola*.

Pastinha became known as the "Philosopher of capoeira" because of his use of many aphorisms. One his favorites was *"Capoeira é para homen, menino e mulher, só não aprende quem não quiser."* ("Capoeira is for men, women and children; the only ones who don't learn it are those who don't wish to.") Like Bimba, he was well versed in the philosophy of *malandragem,* and would tell of how he would carry a small sickle sharpened on both edges in his pocket. "If it had a third edge I would sharpen that one too, for those who wished to do me harm," he was fond of saying.[11]

Unfortunately, government authorities, under the pretext of reforming the Largo do Pelourinho, where he had had his academy, confiscated his class space. Although they promised a new one, they never came through on that promise. The final years of his life were sad: blind and almost abandoned, he lived in a little room until his death in 1981 at the age of ninety-two. He left many pupils, two of the most famous being Mestre João Grande (now teaching in New York) and Mestre João Pequeno.

THE RECENT YEARS

In the 1940s Bahian capoeiristas began to immigrate to Rio, and later to São Paulo and other cities. Nonetheless, until the 1960s,

---

11. As we will see later, Pastinha also spoke of how this blade could be attached to the end of a *berimbau.*

Drawings by Nestor Capoeira, based
on photos of the Senzala group in 1970.
Top: Gato and Mosquito; bottom left: Rafael and Mosquito;
bottom right: Peixinho and Mosquito.

the uncontested mecca for Brazilian capoeiristas continued to be Salvador and the state of Bahia.

In the beginning of the 1960s, capoeira students from Rio's middle class, after studying with Mestre Bimba in Salvador, returned to Rio and began a self-taught apprenticeship. Ten years later, the *Senzala* school reached its apex with the capoeira *rodas* in the neighborhood of Cosme Velho and became the most famous group in Brazil, practicing and teaching a new *Regional-Senzala* style that would influence capoeira players all over the country.

At the same time, in São Paulo there was also a proliferation of capoeira.[12] Intensive warm-ups and systematic practice of blows

---

12. Today that giant metropolis has one of the largest concentration of capoeira academies in Brazil. By one estimate, there are as many as 1,200 academies in the state of São Paulo, many of them concentrated in the capital city.

were added to Bimba's methods. Soon, in Rio as well as in São Paulo, a new cord system inspired by the Asian martial arts was adopted as a means of attracting more students by giving a "clean" image of a new and organized capoeira.

For a while there was even an attempt to create capoeira competitions with championships, judges and rules. Although, at times during the 1970s, it seemed as if capoeira were going to lose its ritualistic, philosophical and game aspects, and turn itself into another among many competitive martial arts, after a few years the championships stopped attracting many of the best capoeiristas. Although such competitions still exist today, they are not generally considered to have any real significance in the capoeira world.

CAPOEIRA IN THE 1970S AND 1980S

In the 1970s and 1980s, capoeira experienced great growth throughout Brazil and for the first time began to expand beyond Brazil's borders. Salvador lost its hegemony or, more accurately, began to share it with Rio and São Paulo due to the migration of its elite young capoeiristas to these two capital cities and the development of strong local capoeira groups there.

In Bahia, the era whose most celebrated elements were Mestre Bimba and Mestre Pastinha came to an end at last.

These two masters and their contemporaries were succeeded by another generation in their sixties and seventies, such as the legendary Mestres Valdemar, Caiçaras, Canjiquinha, João Grande, João Pequeno, Gato, Paulo dos Anjos, Leopoldina, Suassuna, etc.—true connoisseurs and representatives of the capoeira

Mestre Bimba at seventy years of age (drawing by Bodinho).

practiced by the previous generation.

For a while, though, it seemed that the rich and valuable capoeira which they had helped keep alive was rapidly disappearing. Their values, knowledge and philosophy often did not jibe with the new technological era and the new capoeira landscape in which they found themselves, an era in which the individual is alienated and television represents society's highest form of cultural expression—not to mention the drastic changes that occurred in Salvador in the last thirty years, which have to some extent transformed the mystical capital city into a center for consumerism and tourism.

For this reason, one could no longer find the traditional *roda* of Mestre Valdemar in the Liberdade neighborhood. Many of the other mestres, disgusted by this state of affairs, no longer taught, and only very rarely did they play. The mentality had changed; even in the street markets it was hard to see a good player performing.

On the other hand, parallel to this retreat of the traditional *Capoeira Angola* style and its old mestres, the new generation of *Capoeira Regional* teachers that had come from Brazil's middle class were having enormous success in terms of money, number of students, status and media support.

Although capoeira was beginning to experience unparalleled growth and acceptance in Brazilian society, some argued that something was being irrevocably lost along the way.

Muniz Sodre (a.k.a. Americano), a capoeirista from the old guard, warned against these changes in his article "A Brazilian Art of the Body." Capoeira, "as it was practiced by the old mestres from Bahia, was an anti-repressive exercise. To play was a manner of overthrowing the seriousness of the concept of art, established by a neurotic system known as culture."

He continued: "Capoeira today faces subtler and more powerful adversaries: tourism, which changes the ritual into show, and the pedagogical obsession which tries to make of the game and art a sport with rules and regulations."

Inside image: 6 de outubro de 1978   JORNAL DO BRASIL

Nestor Capoeira, herói de corpo fechado em Cordão de Ouro

"CORDÃO DE OURO"

CAPOEIRA E FANTASIA

Article in Jornal do Brasil *announcing the release in 1978 of* Cordão de Ouro, *a film starring Nestor Capoeira.*

CAPOEIRA NOWADAYS – THE 1990S

After the creation of *Capoeira Regional* in Bahia in the 1930s by Mestre Bimba, and the great success of the Senzala group in Rio in the 1960s and '70s, which paralleled the creation of capoeira championships with judges and rules, it seemed that the traditional values of capoeira were seeing their final days. Although a few traditional *Angola* mestres kept on teaching, they were completely eclipsed by the new style that had its origins in Bimba's *Capoeira Regional*.

But unexpectedly, from approximately 1985 onwards, there has been a revival of the traditional *Capoeira Angola*. Fortunately, some of the old mestres were still around, and returned to the capoeira scene with great strength, bringing back roots and values that had seemed completely lost.

Today, we are lucky to find a certain diversity that enriches the capoeira movement. Besides the *Regional/Senzala* style, which brought great technical development in certain kicks and other aspects, we can still find great *Angola* mestres who, along with their own highly developed technique and methods, have added to the deep knowledge of the ritual, music and philosophy of capoeira. And among the new generation of capoeira teachers, who are now around thirty-five years old, we find many of the best interested in both the *Regional/Senzala* style and the traditional *Capoeira Angola* style.

A game of Capoeira Angola *during the famous* roda *of the late Mestre Valdemar (striped shirt).*

O JOGO (THE GAME)

Menino escuta esta toada;
o lance certo muitas vezes esta errado.
Na roda, quem já esta classificado
leva sempre o sorriso que desanuvia
o lábio, ou então um rosto
que é como uma charada.

Hey, young man, listen to this song;
what seems right is often wrong.
In the *roda,* those in the know
always come ready with a smile
that parts their lips, or with an
expression which is but a riddle.

("Menino escuta esta toada"—Nestor Capoeira)

YÊ, VAMOS EMBORA, CAMARÁ!

Imagine that you are in São Salvador, Bahia, Brazil's mystical capital of Afro-Brazilian culture. As you walk through the cobblestone colonial streets of the old part of town, you can feel the pulsating energy that came from Africa centuries ago—an energy which today is the basis for so much of Brazilian culture and everyday life. The weather is hot, and the sun's rays reflect against the blue and green waters of Bahia de Todos os Santos (All Saints' Bay). The light blue sky serves as a stunning backdrop to the pastel-colored houses that line the streets.

People are out in full force—after all, this is not a car-oriented city like so many of today's modern cities. Here the streets and sidewalks serve as a gathering place: a place where people meet, do business, chat, flirt or simply hang out and watch the crowds from one of the many bars that open onto the sidewalk.

As you walk along the streets, suddenly you hear an intriguing sound, barely audible beneath the hum of conversation and laughter. You are lured by this hypnotic music in the distance, and you decide to follow it through the crooked streets.

Suddenly you turn a corner and see a small crowd gathered in a circle. Men, women, teenagers and children all seem to be entranced by what is going on in the center.

You manage to squeeze through the crowd until you get to a small open space in the center. Surrounding this open space are a group of men who are clapping to the beat of the music. Some of them are shirtless, and you can see from the well-defined lines of their upper-body that they are involved in the practice of a very disciplined form of physical activity. At the same time, your intuition tells you that, based on the way they carry themselves, these men are involved in some sort of warrior culture or perhaps even a martial art.

Opposite them you see the percussive band creating the rich sound that first attracted your attention: Three men stand side-by-side, playing long, bow like instruments *(berimbaus),* and they are accompanied by four others playing an assortment of instruments that seem to include a tambourine *(pandeiro)* and a conga drum *(atabaque).*

You are both confused and intrigued. What is this you are witnessing? Is this a dance, or some sort of strange religious ritual? Congratulations, you have just stumbled upon a capoeira *roda* for the first time.

A RODA (THE CIRCLE)

Let us now move closer. Someone begins singing a soulful song, and all listen carefully:

> Boy, who was your mestre?
> My mestre was Solomon.
> I owe him wealth, health and duty.
> I am a disciple who learns
> I am a mestre who teaches.
> The secret of São Cosme,
> is known only to Damon, camará.

"The secret of São Cosme is known only to Damon, camará!"—make no mistake about it: What we have here is a fraternal order, an association whose rites, although openly displayed, have meaning only for those who have been initiated into the mysteries of the game.

> ... Ê arruandê ...

Suddenly you are surprised by the shiver that runs down your spine as you hear the men in the *roda* respond in unison to the singer's call:

> ... *Yê arruandê, camará* ...

Two men are crouched facing each other at the foot of the *berimbau*, with their heads bowed. They seem to be lost in their own thoughts, or perhaps in some form of meditation. They lift their heads and observe the singer as he continues to "lead" the *ladainha*. The chorus responds accordingly as the energy level and the magnetism of the *roda* increase:

> The rooster has crowed;
> —*Yê, the rooster has crowed, camará* . . .
> Ê, co-ro-co-co;
> —*Yê, co-ro-co-co camará* . . .

The singing and the slow, hypnotic rhythm of the *Angola* beat begin to possess the two crouching players. Their minds are free of stray thoughts and ideas. Divested of all extraneous thoughts, they feel as old as the ritual they are about to engage in.

The singer and chorus continue singing in call-and-response fashion:

> Ê, long live my mestre;
> —*Yê, long live my mestre camará* . . .
> Ê, who taught me;
> —*Yê, who taught me, camará* . . .
> Ai, the deceitfulness;
> —*Yê the deceitfulness, camará* . . .
> Ê of capoeira;
> —*Yê of capoeira, camará* . . .

The two men touch the ground with their hands and trace magical signs—sketched lines that "close" the body and strengthen the spirit. The singer continues to lead the *ladainha*, and then gives the signal that the game of capoeira is about to begin:

> Ê, let's go away;
> —*Yê, let's go away, camará* . . .
> Ê, through the wide world;
> —*Yê, through the wide world camará* . . .

Ê, the world goes round;
—*Yê, the world* goes *round camará* . . .
Ê, it went round; . . .
—*Yê it went round, camará* . . .
Ê, it will turn again;
—*Yê, it will turn again camará* . . .

The two players pay their respects at the foot of the *berimbau:*
From a crouched position, they lift their torsos onto their bent arms
while their heads almost touch the ground and their legs hang in
the air. Slowly, with complete control over their bodies, they return
to the initial position and they face each other again. The game has
begun.

They realize that it is no longer their friend or training partner who is in front of them, but instead there stands before them a riddle that can present dangerous and unpredictable enigmas in the corporal dialogue that will follow. It is a dialogue made up not of words but rather of movements—exploratory movements, attack movements, defense movements, deceitful movements—questions and answers in the mysterious language of capoeira.

The players glide to the center of the *roda* with only their hands and feet touching the ground. Their relaxed and seemingly lazy movements contrast with the alertness in their eyes. The singer has finished the soulful chant known as the *ladainha;* the *medio* and *viola berimbaus* improvise and syncopate over the rhythm laid down by the bass *berimbau,* or *gunga.*

The two players are conscious of all of this—the sound of the three *berimbaus,* the beat of the *atabaque,* the *pandeiro.* They observe each other while they effortlessly stand on their heads, make moves reminiscent of a cobra or a cat or a dolphin. They are totally in the moment. Their present and past problems all cease to exist. They observe the moment with a crystal-clear calm and the photographic tranquillity of someone seated on top of a cliff observing the sea.

One of the *berimbau* players leads a new song, still in the slow *Angola* rhythm, and the chorus responds. It is as if all of the energy of the *roda* is channeled and propelled into the pair of players in the center of the *roda.* The energy level continues to rise.

One of the players advances, slowly and carefully, and executes a movement of attack; the other one dodges the kick by moving under it. In spite of the movements that appear to be in slow motion, both players are alert.

Suddenly, one of the players unleashes a kick as quick as a cracking whip. The other, however, anticipates the blow and dodges it effortlessly.

One of the two players spins on his heels and stops with one arm raised. The other one approaches him, swirling close to the ground, and holds one of his adversary's feet in check with his arms so as to prevent any treachery. He cautiously rises and touches his

hand. They walk backward and forward as if engaged in a strange mating ritual, each touching the other's hands ... One of the two breaks this *passo-à-dois* with a quick and sudden kick, but his adversary has already dodged it and is far away.

Now the *berimbaus* start to play at a faster rhythm, called *São Bento Grande,* and the game unfolds standing up. The players swing, break and feint. The blows are swift, violent and unexpected. The defensive movements are dodges, which can be used in turn to set up a counterattack in the form of a kick or a "takedown."

Suddenly, without warning, one of the players spins, stops and carefully approaches his opponent and shakes his hand: This game has ended.

But another pair is already crouching at the foot of the *berimbau;* they pay their respects and a new game begins, with the *berimbau* commanding the rhythm and pace.

A GAME, A FIGHT OR A DANCE?

The question you asked yourself when you first glanced through the crowd comes back to you: Is this a fight or a dance? Or perhaps it was just a *jogo,* a game?

The answer, of course, is that it is all three, and much more.

Capoeira is difficult to define. Somehow the examples just don't fit properly. And it is impossible to classify it in known and established categories—dance, fight, martial art, etc.

To our Western minds, accustomed to dissecting and classifying objects, people and events into specific and standard categories, it can be difficult to grasp and understand what this thing called "capoeira" really is. But if we cut ourselves loose from the demands of our intellectual minds, and just watch the game in the center of the *roda,* we will probably be able to intuitively grasp what is going on here: It is something that we have experienced before, as children, when we played and were completely absorbed by the games that we created with our friends. The key words here are creativity, improvisation, fantasy, beauty and imagination.

But that is not all. Just as important are ritual, danger and sometimes even violence.

So now that we have seen a capoeira *roda* for the first time and have begun to try to define it, let us delve a little further into the matter and explore the three levels of capoeira.

THE THREE LEVELS OF THE GAME

Three seems to be a very popular way of dividing the parts of the whole:

Some speak of the ego, the superego and the id.

Others speak of Brahma, Shiva and Vishnu.

Still others speak of the Father, the Son and the Holy Ghost.

Let us then divide capoeira, for didactic purposes, into three levels.

Keep in mind that these three levels occur simultaneously. However, in any given individual, due to his or her personality, knowledge of the game and level of maturity, one of the three aspects will manifest itself more strongly than the others.

The first level is related to the physical aspects: the fight, the dance and the competition. At this level, it is important to be physically fit, to have efficient and well-placed kicks, to be quick and have good reflexes. On this level, capoeira is an exciting game among warriors.

Most of the players who practice *Capoeira Regional* have developed this aspect to a very high degree, often at the expense of the other two levels.

The player who dwells almost exclusively on this level, though, neglects the ritual of the game, and ignores the roots of capoeira. He does not play the *berimbau* (or plays it poorly); he doesn't sing. He is interested only in playing capoeira, usually in a very methodical way and often in an aggressive manner. He thinks in terms of "winning" or "losing," and he worries about his image and what others will think about him.

As time goes by, the philosophy behind the game begins to seep into the consciousness of the initiate, and he begins to notice a second level to the game—which was always present but which only now can he see and understand clearly.

The first step in understanding this second level is to understand *malícia,* the knowledge of humanity, of life, of the suffering and the motivation and fantasies of human beings.

This is when strange things begin to occur. The sensation of "being there" occurs during a game, shivers run down your spine as you hear the sound of the *berimbau.* The novice slowly begins to learn about the ritual of capoeira: the music, the songs that have been passed down from generation to generation, the philosophy of life of the old mestres. Suddenly it shifts from being a hobby to being part of your day-to-day life. Wining or losing doesn't seem that important anymore, and you are concerned about capoeira as a whole and what you should do to preserve it in the future.

As time goes by, you begin to be seen as an expert, but you realize that you are only a beginner. You begin to see how the practice of capoeira is changing you and your life, and the opportunities that it offers—opportunities to meet new people and to be accepted in new social circles, opportunities to travel all over not as a tourist but as a capoeirista. You also see how it protects you, and makes demands of you as well.

You begin to think about the capoeiristas of the past, and about the odd inheritance passed down from master to student. Sometimes it seems that the game represents something greater, as if it were a reflection of life itself, a reflection of the way different individuals interact with one another, each according to his or her own personality. According to this vision, capoeira is a school where one learns a specific kind of knowledge: how human beings behave toward each other and play the game of life with one another. You feel this odd sensation that something is about to be revealed to you, the feeling you get when someone's name you cannot remember is "at the tip of your tongue."

And then ten, twenty, thirty years go by. You are now a master. There no longer exists any distinction between you and capoeira: You live it; you are one and the same.

You now possess the penetrating glance that is able to discern what goes on between two players, not only on the physical level, but also on the mental and spiritual levels.

You no longer feel the necessity or the urge to experience this or that new or unknown *roda,* and you no longer feel the need to measure yourself against someone who is said to be a great player. You have been around and have seen the "world go round" again and again, and you have established a network of *camarás,* young and old players who are spiritually akin to you and whom you meet again and again throughout the world.

Or perhaps as a consequence of the unfriendly acts and attitudes of your youth, you have become a lone wolf in your later years, admired and respected by the young and inexperienced, but avoided by your peers who have no interest in doing any sort of business with you.

Whatever the case might be, you will then have had access— to a greater or lesser degree—to the third and last level, which had been present all along, since the first day that you heard the sound of a *berimbau,* but which only now reveals itself . . . something that can be called "the mystery and the deceitfulness of the game of life," about which the old mestres tell funny stories and jokes among themselves, but about which they never speak with others because there is nothing to be said to those who do not understand.

MALÍCIA

The *malícia* which the capoeirista refers to is an indispensable trait in the game of capoeira. In capoeira, *malícia* means a mixture of shrewdness, street-smarts, and wariness. It should not be confused with the English word "malice."

It may be said that *malícia* has two basic aspects. The first is knowing the emotions and traits—aggressiveness, fear, pride, vanity, cockiness, etc.—which exist within all human beings. The second is recognizing these traits when they appear in another player, and therefore being able to anticipate the other player's movements, whether in the *roda* or in everyday life. The player who is *malicioso* is able to dodge under an opponent's kick and prepare for a counterattack or a takedown before the assailant finishes what he started. In everyday life, he should be able to recognize the real human being that hides beneath the social mask of someone he has just met.

Another aspect of *malícia* consists of deceiving or faking the opponent into thinking that you are going to execute a certain move when in fact you are going to do something completely different and unexpected.

The development of *malícia* is a never-ending process that is stimulated by playing the game itself, by observing others as they play capoeira, and by observing everyday events in our lives and in the lives of others.

Malícia sometimes is called *mandinga,* although the latter word has an even broader meaning, since it also implies that one understands the basic forces of nature and knows how to use them to a certain extent by means of rituals involving magic.

Although an understanding of *malícia* and *mandinga* are essential to becoming a capoeirista, many players get carried away with it in the greater scheme of things. They forget a popular Brazilian saying, *"Malandro demais se atrapalha,"* which means that when one tries to be too clever or smart, instead of confusing his opponent, he confuses himself. They lose their way as they come into contact with this type of knowledge. They get obsessed with being smart, smarter than others, and with being powerful, more powerful than others; they get obsessed with being famous and with having status. And they forget that we all belong to the same *roda,* and that one has to have friends, one has to have fun, one has to enjoy the company of other human beings, in order to get the most out of life.

THE ORIGINS OF MALÍCIA: THE SLAVE AND THE BANDIT

We have already given a poetic description of the city of Salvador and of the capoeira *roda,* and that gives us a good insight into the "game." But if we are really going to begin to understand capoeira we must also have another picture of it and of its Brazilian environment. Let us then visit the neighborhood of one of the most famous mestres in Rio de Janeiro.

Demerval Lopes de Lacerda, better known as mestre Leopoldina, is famous for his quick and very unique style of playing capoeira, as well as for his mastery of the *berimbau.* But above all he is famous for the songs that he composes, which are sung wherever there is a capoeira *roda.*

Leopoldina must be well into his sixties, but nobody knows his exact age. If you ask him, he will tell you that he is exactly 283 years old and that Zumbi, who was the famous leader of a *quilombo* (a village built in the jungle by runaway Africans who were enslaved from the sixteenth to the nineteenth centuries), had been his pupil and that Besouro, a celebrated capoeirista who lived in the beginning of the century, was his second-in-command in a capoeira *roda* held in the city of Santo Amaro.

Cidade de Deus, the part of Rio where Leopoldina lives, is quite a fantastic place. It is not exactly a *favela,* one of the shantytowns or slums that line the many beautiful hills gently squeezing the town against the sea. Cidade de Deus has certain amenities that one does not find in the *favelas,* such as sewer, gas and water lines.

Also, the streets are paved and it is not on a hillside. But other than that, the social and cultural environment is pretty much the same as in a *favela*. That means that authority here does not lie with the state or federal government or even with the police, who must plan a special incursion with at least forty or fifty heavily armed men just to go into the area.

Law and authority here are concentrated in one person—the man in charge of cocaine and marijuana trafficking—and the hundred or more persons that he commands.

Although Cidade de Deus is a small part of Rio de Janeiro in the 1990s, it is a good insight into the slums that exist in all big Brazilian cities, not only in our day but also as it must have been in the last century. Let us not forget that the gangs that rule the drug scenes today live in the same *favela* that housed the capoeira gangs at the end of the nineteenth century. The social situation has remained very much the same since then.

At that time, a very small portion of society made up of the Portuguese rulers and their descendants born in Brazil controlled nearly all the riches and power. We also had a slightly bigger part of society represented by what is today called the middle class, and finally an enormous mass of slaves made up of free men and women captured in Africa, and their descendants who were born into slavery in Brazil.

After Brazil became independent from Portugal it was the same aristocratic group that maintained power; for it was Pedro I, son of the Portuguese King João VI, who took his father's advice to take the power for himself before another opportunist could do so, and made Brazil independent.

In theory Brazil was independent from Portugal, but in practice it was completely under the economic rule of England, Portugal's European ally, which had a monopoly on imports and exports to and from Brazil. In the early 1900s, after World War I, and later on, after World War II, this same economic and political and social model was maintained, although the domination was no longer English but American.

Now, in the final years of the twentieth century, we still have the same basic model, with the domination exercised by the big trans-national or multi-national economic groups. Nothing, in fact, has changed much: Brazil is the tenth most powerful economy in the world, and at the same time it is third in the list of countries with the most unfair and perverted distribution of money and wealth. A great part of Brazil's income from exports goes directly into the hands of international and North American banks and funds like the IMF (International Monetary Fund) to pay the enormous debt that Brazil's government has accumulated since the 1950s, the bulk of which was incurred between 1964 and 1984, during the period that the military took power.

Why are we telling you all of this? It is only under this global view that it is possible to understand the corruption and lawlessness that exist in the Third World. And it is only by considering this perspective that we can understand the unwritten rules and bizarre ethics of capoeira.

Capoeira is the culture of the oppressed! It was created in Brazil, sometime in the eighteenth or nineteenth centuries, by men enslaved in Africa and brought to Brazil. It was further developed by men living in the underworld of banditry and on the margins of an extremely unfair society during the 19th and 20th centuries.

Only after 1934 was the practice of capoeira permitted, and only then did it begin to come out from underground and to be practiced by individuals from more privileged social groups. Even then, there was a stigma attached to capoeira and its past, a stigma that began to fade only in the 1960s and 1970s.

From the very beginning, capoeira had to struggle to survive, since all African cultural activity was repressed in the 1800s. Facing a stronger opponent who controlled the power and made the laws, capoeira had to learn to be flexible and avoid frontal confrontations, to go with the flow of things. Capoeira learned the guerrilla way of fighting when faced by a stronger and more established army. It learned the value of lies and deceit, of ambush, surprise and treason.

One does not block a kick in capoeira; on the contrary, one goes along with it, thus avoiding the blow, and then counterattacking if possible. One does not confront a man face to face, but rather pretends to be a coward, to ask for mercy—and then to hit the opponent when he lowers his guard.

Capoeira knows nothing of such words, valued in Western society, as honesty, truth and fairplay when facing the enemy. Such concepts are luxuries that are not available when you are slave to a master who goes to church in the morning and at night rapes young women in the slave quarters, not even considering them to be human beings but simply *peças* (literally pieces, or units with some economic value). In the capoeirista's world view, such concepts are to be employed only with those who have proved real friendship.

On the other hand, it was clearly understood by the enslaved Africans, and later by the bandits, that one should not merely prepare oneself to objectively win or survive. Life is much more than just winning or surviving—it involves the joy of being alive. So all of this —music, dance, creativity, improvisation, poetry, philosophy, and having fun—is part of capoeira too.

But what about the First World? Has capoeira, with its special ethics and way of being, any value for Europeans or North Americans? Here the situation is quite different, for a good part of the population has achieved an economic level that permits them to live in a reasonably comfortable way. But economic and material well-being are not enough. Life, as we said before, is far greater than that.

In that sense, capoeira can be a tool in the First World, a tool against the forces that tend to turn people into robots that do not think, do not wish, do not have any fantasies, ideals, imagination or creativity; a tool against a civilization that increasingly says one simply has to work and then go home and sit in front of a TV with a can of beer in hand, like a pig being fattened for the slaughterhouse.

THE MUSIC

My *berimbau* . . .
whosoever should hear it play,
their sorrow, the sorrow they feel, will disappear.
You shall create a soul that is always new,
you shall create a soul that is always new!
My *berimbau* . . .
but whosoever should hear it play,
if it be a maid, she will become engaged.
My *berimbau*,
he only brings happiness, my comrade,
Yê, é hora, é hora . . .

     (*"Louvação do Berimbau,"* by Mestre Leopoldina)

MUSIC AND CAPOEIRA

The capoeira *roda* consists of the following major instruments: a *berimbau*, an *atabaque* and a *pandeiro*. It can also include other instruments which are often present but which are not indispensable for most *rodas:* the *reco-reco* and the *agô-gô* (cow-bell).[13]

THE BERIMBAU

There is much lore surrounding the *berimbau:*

- Mestre Pastinha tells how, in the old days, a small sickle sharpened on both sides would be attached to the end of the instrument in order to create a deadly weapon: "In the moment of truth it would cease to be a musical instrument and would turn into a hand sickle." Thus the instrument, like the game of capoeira itself, combined within it two antagonistic poles: music and death, dance and fight, beauty and violence.

- It is said that in certain parts of Africa it was forbidden for the young who cared for the livestock to play this instrument; it was thought that its sound would take the soul of the youth—which was still inexperienced—to the "land of no return."

- In Cuba, where it is known as *burumbumba,* it is used to communicate with the spirit of the dead ancestors (*eguns*) in ceremonies of necromancy (Fernando Ortiz, *Los*

---

13. *The traditional Angola roda* usually requires three berimbaus (high-tone, mid-tone and bass), and one or more *pandeiro,* plus the *atabaque,* the *reco-reco* and the *agô-gô.* However, depending on the *roda* and on the ritual followed by the local mestre, some will do without these last three instruments.

Instrumentos de la Musica Afro-Cubana, Dirección de Cultura del Ministerio de Educación, Havana, 1952).

• The *berimbau* was also used in many parts of Africa and Brazil during the nineteenth century to accompany chants, storytelling and poetry (Debret, *Voyage Pittoresque et Historique au Brèsil,* Firmin Didot Frères, Paris, 1834).

The *berimbau* creates the mood and dictates the rhythm and nature of the game taking place within the *roda*. According to the old mestres, "The *berimbau* teaches."

Along with the hand-clapping, the chants, the *pandeiro* and the *atabaque,* the *berimbau* influences the players' actions inside of the *roda*. Or, if you prefer, these attract forces and energies to the *roda* which vary according to the beat chosen.

The *berimbau* is made of a wooden bow, approximately seven palm-lengths long and three quarters to one inch in diameter.

Berimbau *player (Debret 1834).*

At its widest end, a small peg is carved on which to attach a steel wire. The other extremity is covered by a leather patch, which prevents the wire from penetrating and cracking the wood. Nowadays the wire is taken from the inner sides of old car tires.[14]

A dry, hollowed-out gourd, called a *cabaça* in Portuguese, serves as a percussive box to amplify the sound of the instrument. A wide circular opening is made where the stem of the fruit used to be, and on the opposite side there are two small perforations threaded by a ring of string which is used to fasten the gourd to the bow.

The *berimbau* is usually held in the left hand along with a stone, a coin or a metal washer (*vintém*), which produces one of two notes produced by the instrument, depending on whether or not it is touching the metal wire.

The sound of the *berimbau* is produced when the wire is struck by a wooden stick (*baqueta*) approximately twelve inches long, which is held in the right hand along with a small shaker (*caxixi*) made of woven straw. The sound of the dried beans or pebbles inside the *caxixi* enriches and adds texture to the *berimbau's* sound.

By either placing or removing the gourd on the abdomen, the player can obtain different modulations of the same basic notes. There are three types of *berimbaus,* and ideally all are present in the *roda:*[15]

- The *gunga*, which has the deepest sound, plays the role of the bass; it keeps the rhythm, and normally plays the basic theme of a certain beat without variations.

- The *berimbau médio,* or *de centro*, also known simply as the *berimbau*, plays over the basic rhythm of the *gunga;* it plays a

---

14. In the old days, animal entrails were used.

15. Mestre Bimba would generally use only one *berimbau* in the roda, and he did so in his LP record *"Curso de Capoeira Regional."* When he is singing and the chorus is answering, we see that he played his *berimbau* as the *médio* that it was (he plays the basic theme of the *São Bento Grande,* followed by the basic variation of that beat, again and again). But between songs he improvises as if his *berimbau* were a *violinha.*

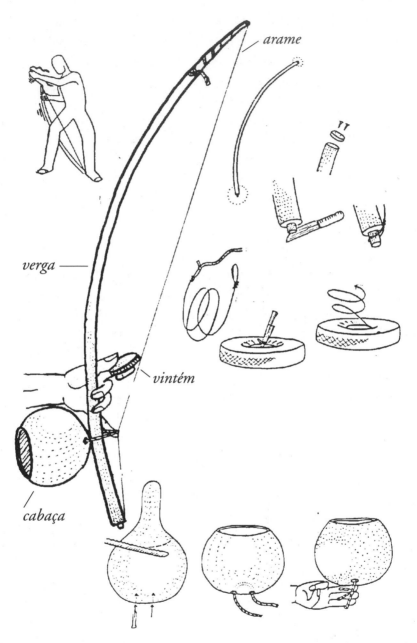

arame

verga

vintém

cabaça

The making of a berimbau. Wire is removed from the inside of a tire, and a gourd is cut in the fashion shown above, to serve as a percussive box which amplifies the sound of the instrument.

role similar to that of the rhythm guitar. For example, it can play the basic theme of a certain beat, then a basic variation on it, and then return to the basic theme, and so on.

• The *viola* or *violinha* is the *berimbau* that has the sharpest sound; it is responsible for the syncopation or the improvisation. The role that it plays is equivalent to the solos of a lead guitar.[16]

The richness and intricacy of the rhythms make up for whatever melodic limitations the *berimbau* might have—when it is in the hands of an experienced player, one would never suspect it has only two notes.

The movements by the players inside the *roda* reflect the rhythms played. Depending on the rhythms or beats being played, the game can be either slow and treacherous, fast and aggressive, or open and harmonious.

There are many beats to choose from. Some are universal, such as *Angola, São Bento Pequeno, São Bento Grande.* Others are peculiar to one region or another, or were created by various persons. That is the case of the rhythms played by practitioners of *Capoeira Regional,* who play to the rhythms created by Mestre Bimba—*São Bento Grande (de Regional), Cavalaria (de Regional), Iúna, Amazonas,* etc.

THE CHANTS

The chants are not merely an accompaniment to the rhythms created by the *berimbau;* singing along with others in the *roda* is essen-

---

16. The use of three instruments with deep, medium and high-pitched sound is used in many African musical structures. We find it in *candomblé* (Afro-Brazilian religion), where three types of drums are used, except that the deep-sounding drum improvises (instead of the high-pitched *berimbau,* which improvises in capoeira). We also find this structure in Western music that has roots in African culture, such as rock-and-roll ("grandson of the blues") with the bass, rhythm and solo guitar.

tial to creating the necessary energy level required for the games to unfold and manifest themselves in the deepest and most complete way.

Also, within the three basic types of chants or *chulas*—the *ladainha*, the *quadras* and the *corridos*—there can be found a series of teachings, a code of conduct and the basic premises of a philosophical world view.[17] The *ladainha* is sung by the "soloist" before the start of a game, and is followed by a second part which is answered by the "chorus." *Quadras* are four-verse songs sung by the soloist and answered by the chorus. *Corridos* are one- or two-verse songs sung by the soloist and answered by the chorus.

If it can be said that "the *berimbau* teaches"—as the old mestres like to say—its teachings would be directed at the deepest reaches of the human consciousness.

But with the chants we find another, more rational type of teaching, based on the life experience of the elderly practitioners of this game. Let us examine a few verses of the *chulas:*

> *No Céu entra quem merece,*
> *Na Terra vale é quem tem.*
> *Passar bem ou passar mal,*
> *Tudo na vida é passar, camará.*

You enter heaven on your merits;
Here on Earth what you own is all that counts.
Fare you well or fare you poorly,
All on this Earth is but farewell, comrade.

(Traditional capoeira song)

* * *

---

17. The *ladainhas* usually "open" or begin the *roda*. They are typical of Capoeira Angola.

Ê! Maior é Deus!
Ê! Maior é Deus!
Pequeno sou eu.
O que eu tenho foi Deus quem me deu.
Na roda da capoeira
Grande e pequeno sou eu.

Ê! God is greater!
Ê! God is greater!
Little am I.
What I have God gave me.
In the capoeira *roda*,
Both great and small am I.

(Mestre Pastinha)

Many songs are of unknown origin; others, however, are written by very well-known capoeiristas:

A lei de Murici:
Cada um trata de si.

The law of Murici:
I'm looking out for me.

(Mestre Leopoldina)

* * *

Não seja vaidoso
Nem precepitado.

Be you neither vain
Nor be you rash.

(Mestre Pastinha)

* * *

Era Bimba, era Pastinha,
Era Besouro e Abêrrê
Que jogavam capoeira
Como seu modo de ver.

There was Bimba, there was Pastinha,
There was Besouro and Abêrrê,
All who used to play capoeira,
All in their very own way.

(Mestre Lua)

Other songs speak about the atmosphere of criminality in which capoeira was born and developed:

Meu patrão sempre me dizia
Não fume desse negócio.
Se é de madrugada,
é arma de fogo e velório.

My boss would always tell me
Don't smoke any of that stuff.
If it's late at night,
You're talking firearm and a deathwatch.

(Mestre Bimba)

Then there are the songs that relate stories of encounters with "enchanted ones," with people who are possessed, and with the devil himself:

Tava lá no pé da cruz
Fazendo minha oração
Quando chegou Dois-de-ouro
Como a figura do Cão.

There I was at the foot of the cross,
Saying my prayer,

When *Dois-de-ouro*[18] arrived
Like the figure of the Dog.[19]

In W. Rego's excellent book entitled *Capoeira Angola* (mentioned earlier) we find many interesting chants such as this one:

Riachão tava cantando
Na cidade de Açu
Quando apareceu um negro
Da espécie do urubu.

Riachão was singing
In the city of Açu,
When a Negro arrived
Of the vulture kind.

In this song, the "Negro of the vulture kind" challenges Riachão to sing and improvise verses with him. Later it is revealed that he is the devil himself.

As is only natural for a game that is part of the vast and complex whole of Afro-Brazilian culture, many chants allude to *candomblé* deities, many times by the name of their corresponding Catholic saint. *Candomblé* is one of the religions the Africans brought to Brazil from their home continent, and it can be found in Brazil in its almost pure African form as well as mixed with native Indian and European cultures. *Candomblé* is the cult of the *orixas* (*ori* = head, *xá* = strength), or *orishas,* the cosmic energies that rule humans, the world and life itself.[20]

These *orixas* constitute a pantheon of gods similar to the ones we find in other ancient cultures such as the Scandinavian Viking

---

18. Two of diamonds; famous capoeirista.

19. Nickname for the devil.

20. Although *candomblé* is something apart from capoeira, in the past most capoeira players belonged to that religion. That is the reason we find so many references to it in capoeira songs.

culture or the classical Greek and Roman cultures. This song is an example:

> *Santo Antonio é protetor da barquinha de Noé,*
> *ê, da barquinha de Noé.*

> Saint Anthony is the protector of Noah's little ark,
> ê, of Noah's little ark.

Here the song speaks of "Saint Anthony" in the context of the biblical ark, but, in fact, it is referring to Ogun, the god of battles and war who is also the deity associated with iron.

> *Ai, ai, ai, ai, São Bento me chama.*

> Ai, ai, ai, ai, Saint Bento is calling me.

Saint Bento is said to protect against snake bites, and it is also the name given to two *berimbau* rhythms, São Bento Pequeno and São Bento Grande.

Among all the animals, the snake is the most celebrated one in capoeira songs, maybe because of its flexibility, and the fact that when it attacks it is quick, precise, treacherous and lethal. Here is one of the many songs that make reference to snakes:

> *Olha a cobra que morde*
> *Senhor São Bento.*

> Watch out for the snake that bites,
> Senhor São Bento.

It is very common for songs to guide the action of the players inside the *roda:*

> *Ai, ai, Aidê, joga bonito que eu quero ver ...*
> *Joga bonito que eu quero aprender.*

> Ai, ai, Aidê, play pretty 'cause I want to see ...
> Play pretty 'cause I want to learn.

And to leave no doubt that the chants reflect the action inside the *roda,* one needs only to hear the lyrics to the following chant:

Cabra correu com medo de apanhar ...
correu, correu com medo de apanhar.

The guy ran, scared of getting clobbered ...
He ran, he ran, scared of getting clobbered.

Another less obvious but equally important aspect of these chants is to allow the capoeira player who has just arrived at a *roda* to easily bring his energy in tune with the energy of those already there. He is thus able to relax and unwind the tensions accumulated throughout the day.

A more subtle function performed by the chants is that they allow players to catch their breath. Just like the swimmer who raises and dips his head in a rhythmic breathing pattern, the participants in a *roda* are also forced to enter a rhythmic breathing pattern as they respond in chorus fashion to the chants that others are leading. After finishing a game, many times tired and breathless, singing in chorus is a wonderful way to catch your breath!

LEARNING CAPOEIRA

Sou disípulo que aprende,
Sou mestre que dá lição.

I am a disciple that learns,
I am a mestre that teaches

TABLE OF CONTENTS
FOR MOVEMENTS AND KICKS

Movement 61

  1. The ginga 62

  2. The negativa and rolê 65

  3. The aú 69

Defensive Movements 71

  1. The cocorinha 71

  2. The resistencia 72

  3. Queda de quatro 72

  4. The esquiva 73

The Basic Kicks 73

  1. Meia lua de frente 74

  2. Armada 75

  3. Queixada 77

  4. Martelo-do-chão 78

  5. Chapa-de-costas 79

  6. Benção 80

  7. Martelo-em-pé 81

  8. Meia lua de compasso 83

Bimba's Sequences 86

  First sequence 88

  Second sequence 91

  Third sequence 94

  Fourth sequence 97

  Fifth sequence 99

Sixth sequence 101

Seventh sequence 103

Eighth sequence 105

Cintura Desprezada 106

Takedowns 108

1. Rasteira 109

2. Banda 111

3. Negativa derrubando 112

4. Negativa with tesoura 113

5. Arrastão 114

6. Boca de calça 115

7. Boca de calça de costas 116

8. Cruz 117

9. Banda por dentro 118

10. Banda de costa 119

11. Açoite de braço 120

12. Tesoura 121

13. Tesoura de frente 122

14. Vingativa 123

15. Tombo-de-ladeira 124

Other Kicks and Movements 124

1. Chapa-de-frente 125

2. Cruzado 126

3. S-dobrado 126

4. Chibata 127

5. Ponteira 128

6. Vôo-do-morcego 128

7. Macaco 129

8. Meia lua pulada 129

9. Compasso 130

10. Chapeu-de-couro 131

11. Rabo-de-arraia 131

12. Armada with martelo 132

13. Arpão de cabeça 132

14. Escorumelo 133

15. Asfixiante 133

16. Galopante 134

17. Godeme 134

18. Cutelo 134

19. Cutuvelda 134

20. Dedeira 134

21. Telefone 135

The Language of Angola 135

Passo-à-dois 136

Chamada de cocorinha 137

Passagem de tesouras 137

Saída para o jogo 138

Volta do mundo 138

Queda de rins 138

"I am a disciple that learns, I am a master that teaches." This quote from a well-known capoeira song reveals one of the most interesting and unique *fundamentos* (philosophical roots) of capoeira: The *capoeirista* always plays the dual role of both teacher and student, regardless of whether he is a beginner or an eighty-year-old master. He is always a pupil who is learning in the *roda* and in life, and he is always a teacher who is teaching, both in the *roda* and in life.

In fact, the real learning in capoeira occurs during the interaction between players during the *roda,* and not in the more structured instruction sessions. In the *roda,* players learn from each other—not only moves and kicks, but also strategies that are used in the game itself or in the bigger "game" that we play everyday in "real" life.

The players learn from each other, and those who are watching learn in turn from them. These varied observations of different personalities interacting with one another constitute an important body of knowledge about human beings, knowledge which also constitutes the *fundamento* or philosophical root called *malícia.*

In the "good old days"—which most likely were not so good— capoeira was learned naturally and intuitively; one would observe movements in the *roda* and try to imitate those movements. If one was lucky, one would find a mestre. Wherever a mestre would go, he would be followed by two or three apprentices. Now and then the mestre would give a pointer, and teach something.

Nowadays, times have changed. People have very little free time available. Mestres can no longer can be found wandering about. There are not many street *rodas* left where one can learn by trial and error in an intuitive, organic way. Capoeira nowadays is taught in the academies, each instructor teaching according to his own methods.

In the *Regional* academies, the teaching methods tend to be very structured; this permits a rapid development of technique, often to the detriment of improvisation, spontaneity and exploration of a player's individuality.

In the *Angola* academies, whose enrollments have been growing since 1985 after many years of being eclipsed by the *Regional* style, the teachings are more intuitive. The *Angoleiro* is almost always more flexible, has more *malícia,* and improvises more. Nonetheless, in the short run, the *Angoleiro* has a disadvantage, since the standardized technique and teaching method represent a decided advantage for the *Regional* players in the first years of instruction.

With the exception of traditional *Angola* mestres, plus two or three pupils of Bimba who are now in their fifties and who try to teach the original *Capoeira Regional,* what is now being taught in most academies throughout Brazil is a capoeira that could be called *Regional/Senzala,* because they use teaching methods developed by the Senzala group during the 1960s. These in turn build on the teaching methods developed by Mestre Bimba.

Thus, in today's classes, we see a lot of sequences of predetermined blows designed for two players which resemble Bimba's sequence. We also see systematic repetition of blows and movements done by many students at the same time as they follow the instructor's lead (similar to what we observe in the Eastern martial arts). And during the last thirty years or so, we have also seen the addition of calisthenic exercises, gymnastic and stretching techniques.

Nowadays we also see young *Angola* instructors who are teaching *Angola* but using methods similar to *Regional/Senzala,* with predetermined sequences of blows and movements as well as methodical repetition.

The ideal for a player who is already very advanced in his learning is to know and to practice both styles:

- to play *Angola,* with all of its ritual and *malícia;* and

- to play *Regional* (more accurately, *Regional/Senzala*), with its objectivity and its fighting spirit.

The beginner, however, in order to aid in his development, would do well to heed some of the pithy popular proverbs that are the essence of the *malandragem* philosophy—sayings such as *"Quem não pode com mandinga não carrega patúa."* ("He who can't deal with the *mandinga* doesn't carry a *patúa*."[21]) In other words, everyone should know his or her limits. Or: *"Urubu para cantar demora."* ("A vulture takes a long time to sing.") Another version of this is: *"Bater papo com otário é jogar conversa fora."* ("Chatting with a fool is a waste of words.")

Of all of the proverbs, though, perhaps the best one for the beginner to keep in mind is that *"valente não existe,"* which can be translated as "There's no such thing as a tough guy" or "the fearless do not exist." It is important for the beginner not to be fooled by the outward appearance of some "tough guys," and to realize that we all feel fear, and that we are all—to greater and lesser extents—insecure: "The fearless do not exist."

The capoeira player needs to see the human being hidden behind the facade of physical strength, whether it be in himself or in others. If this does not occur, then the beginner will guide his studies by a series of false precepts and stereotypical ideas, such as the macho tough guy, the deadly blow, or the notion of the superiority of one fighting art over another.

As time goes by, the beginner who guides himself by these false notions will turn into an idol of clay feet, an edifice with a weak base; he will have faith in the fighting techniques but not in the fighter; he will have powerful blows but lack faith in the person who delivers those blows; he will develop his muscles and his technique but not his spiritual strength. On the street, he will be able to beat this or that guy—but he will have to do this ever more frequently to reaffirm to himself and to others the image he is trying to impose. And once he runs into someone with a hot temperament and a cool head, he will crumble with the fear that his great

---

21. Magic amulets usually worn around the neck as a protection against evil and injury.

farce will be revealed for what it is.

In this increasingly violent sequence of events, he might feel the necessity to walk around with a gun, and he will then notice that others are also carrying guns. And the painful progression of his paranoia will be never-ending, transforming him into a coward who kisses up to the strong and the violent. It will transform him into the weakest of tyrants. All of this will occur because he didn't have the courage to look within himself and those that he idolized, because he was unable to see the human being within, in all of its manifestations both positive and negative.

PRESENTATION OF MOVEMENTS

We now leave behind the first part of the book, which dealt with theory. Let us now begin the section where beginning students are given a method of learning how to *jogar,* or play capoeira.

What makes this method a bit different from the methods that are being used nowadays and that have been used in the last fifty years (since Bimba created the *Regional* teaching method) is that it tries to combine the creativity and improvisation typical of *Capoeira Angola* with the structured and methodical training techniques of *Regional/Senzala,* which brought about great development in kicking techniques but unfortunately often made a player's movements resemble those of a mechanical robot.

We propose to do this by introducing the reader to a series of training techniques for movements of attack and defense through the use of diagrams and specific, concrete instructions and explanations.

When beginning any apprenticeship, the beginner often feels clumsy and foolish. He is full of good intentions, but after the first attempts he becomes discouraged. The student often rationalizes his difficulties by saying "I'm not cut out for this," and considers giving up.

This is normal in any learning process. However, we should try to educate ourselves so that we may overcome this inertia, this resistance, this fear of the new.

The beginner should allow himself ten initial lessons in which he puts aside all rationalizations and excuses for not studying and learning capoeira. I believe that after those first lessons the student will begin seeing things differently, and will realize that learning capoeira in order to play and be part of the *roda* is much easier and more fun than he initially thought. Of course, if he then wishes to achieve a high level of proficiency in capoeira, it will mean many years of practice and dedication.

Classes usually last one-and-a-half to two hours, three to five times a week. After the first six months the student should have conquered the first level of learning—he is now capoeira-literate.

I highly recommend that in the beginning students start with a master or a teacher who can guide them in the right direction. This is especially true outside of Brazil, where capoeira is just beginning to take off, and you cannot live and breathe capoeira as you can in Brazil.

It is also essential for the reader to keep in mind that capoeira is not merely the execution of moves and kicks. The final objective is to be able to *jogar,* or to play capoeira, and to do this you need other players.

THE MOVEMENT

Movement is basic to capoeira. Most beginners, and many advanced players, do not pay enough attention to this aspect of capoeira; they become so fascinated with learning different kicks or flashy new acrobatic flips that they forget this essential part of the game.

Let us explore three basic elements of movement in capoeira:

- the *ginga*—a form of movement standing up.

- the *negativa* and the *rolê*—forms of movement on the floor.

- the *aú*—a form of upside-down movement.

These movements are so important that I suggest that, before learning any kicks, the beginner set aside three classes just to explore them.

Students should seek out smoothness and harmony in their movements, and put aside the notion that they are studying a fighting style—this notion will only cause the beginner to tense up, and will cause his movements to be rigid, which is totally antithetical to capoeira.

The following exercise should be done to the slow rhythm of *Angola,* and some will gradually speed up to the rhythm of *São Bento Grande.* For those unfamiliar with the tempo of those two rhythms, we could say that the first corresponds to soulful blues and the latter to a frenzied boogie-woogie.

1. THE GINGA
(pronounced "jinga")

The *ginga* is one of the basic movements of capoeira. It is one of the features that sets capoeira apart from all other martial arts. Roughly translated, it means "swing" in English.

What makes the *ginga* special as compared to other martial art stances is that it puts capoeiristas in constant motion, making them a very frustrating target for an opponent.

The importance of the *ginga* cannot be overstressed. From the ginga the capoeirista can hide, dodge, feint and attack.

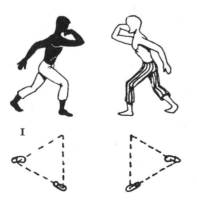

As a general rule, the *ginga* in *Capoeira Angola* is very free and individualistic. The ginga in *Regional,* on the other hand, is very structured, and its basic steps can actually be shown in a diagram form. This basic structure, however, does not mean that a *Regional* player cannot add his own style to these moves as he begins to master them.

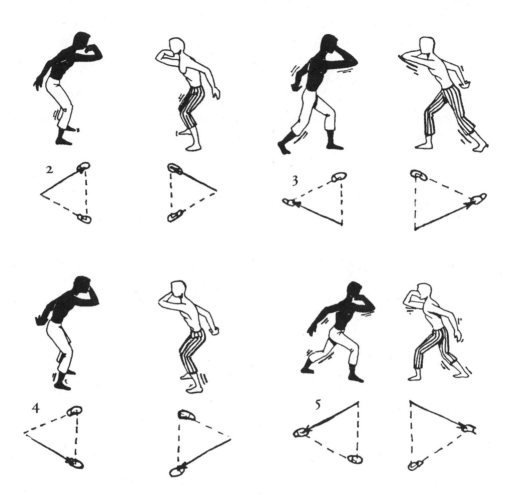

Exercises:

a) *Ginga* alone, as shown in the diagrams until you have assimilated the basic movements of the ginga.

b) *Ginga* facing another person, one following the ginga of the other as if looking at a mirror.

c) Movement improvisation (standing up): Now forget about the *ginga* and just move around your partner. Try to go around him. Avoid moving directly into him or cutting his movements short. Improvise your movements, and don't be ashamed of looking ridiculous. Your partner should do the same thing.

In this exercise, don't worry about synchronizing your movements with your partner. Forget briefly any preconceived notions that you may have about fighting. Relax and enjoy the dialogue of movements between you and your partner.

Move freely and try to react to each of his moves without throwing any kicks. Do not use the basic ginga in this part of the exercise; rather, use your instincts and your wits—you will find that they serve you well in capoeira!

Try to encircle your partner, putting him in the middle of a web of movements. This exercise is fundamental to avoiding a mechanical and robotlike *ginga,* which unfortunately is a trademark of many capoeiristas nowadays. Later we will explore movements of improvisation on the floor. These exercises are the core of this teaching method, and special attention should be paid to them.

d) Do the basic *ginga* alone. Then work with the improvised movements you did above by moving forward, backward, laterally and around. While improvising in this way, do not use the basic *ginga* movement. But after each series of improvised movements, return to the basic *ginga.* Eventually, this transition from improvisation to basic *ginga* movement should be seamless, so that an observer cannot tell when one begins and the other ends. Don't be tense; be relaxed and flowing. Let your arms flow along with you while you move. For now, do not put them in a fighting position.

e) Repeat the above exercises with a partner. When improvising, attempt to go around your opponent and to react to his movements. He will in turn react to your movements. Have a dialogue.

Note: With exercises a) and b), you will structure your basic ginga in the *Regional* style shown in the diagram. With exercise c) you will start developing your own personal way of moving while interacting or playing with someone else. With exercise d) you will start to articulate your personal way of moving, and blend it in with the basic capoeira *ginga.* And with e) you are going to play and interact with another person using your own personal way of moving blended with the basic capoeira *ginga.*

It is extremely important to understand how these five steps lead to learning the *ginga,* and the way that they relate to one another, if you expect to profit from the method presented here. This method combines the positive innovations brought about by Bimba's teaching method (combined with the contribution of the *Senzala* method developed in the sixties) with the creative and improvisational characteristics that are typical of the traditional *Angola* method of teaching.

If you understand how this is applied to the *ginga,* then you will have a clear insight into all of the other teaching methods and exercises presented in the following pages.

2. THE NEGATIVA AND THE ROLÊ
(pronounced "ho-lay")

Another distinguishing feature of capoeira with respect to most other martial arts is that the capoeirista is very adept at moving on the floor. Just as the *ginga* is the basic movement of the capoeirista when standing, the *negativa* and the *rolê* are his basic form of movement on the floor.

When the players move on the floor, they touch the ground only with their hands and feet, and eventually with their heads. They do not touch the ground with their knees, or roll onto their backs.

Going to the floor and moving there is part of the web of unexpected movements that dazzles the opponent. But the experienced player can also go to the floor in a real fight situation in order to lure his opponent into thinking that he is vulnerable and not realizing that a trap has been set for him. There exist a great number of kicks and takedowns meant to be used specifically in such situations.[22]

Last, but not least, moving on the floor makes the capoeirista familiar with the floor in such a way that he can quickly recover from a fall or even an attack, or take down his opponent from the floor.

---

22. Exercises for such situations are directed towards experienced players, and will be presented in Nestor's second book.

Regional *negativa*

Angola *negativa*

Coming up from the *negativa* with a *rolê*

Another way of standing up from the *negativa*

The *Regional negativa* is more erect; in *Angola* it is usually closer to the ground. The *rolê* can also be used as the transition from the *negativa* to the *ginga,* or from the floor to a standing position. In the diagrams we can see another form of "coming up" from the *negativa*.

Exercises:

a) Approach your training partner using the *rolê* while he stands still.

b) Move away from your partner using the *rolê*.

c) *Ginga,* go down into the *negativa*, change legs in the *negativa* so that your other legs is extended. (Important: Put weight on the hand that is on the floor when you switch legs, so that you spare your knees. Once you have switched legs, then proceed to switch your hands.)

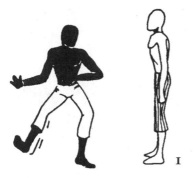
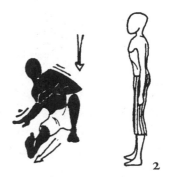

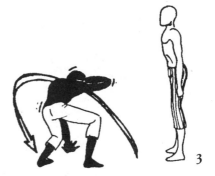

Moving away in *negativa* and *rolê*

d) After having changed legs in the *negativa,* try approaching your partner while he stands still.

e) Execute various *rolês* in a row.

f) Move on all fours, like a cat. Move forward and backward.

g) Move along the floor with one hand always touching the ground, like a monkey.

h) Move freely on the floor, occasionally using the *rolê* and changing legs in the *negativa.*

Note: In all of the above exercises, only the hands and feet should touch the floor.

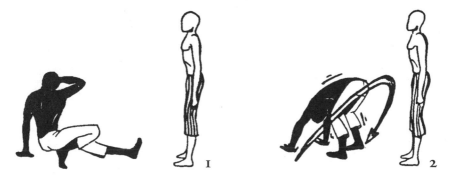

Approaching in *negativa* and *rolê*

i) Movement improvisation (on the ground): a transition from the *negativa* (a) to the *ginga* position (f) by executing the *rolê* (b,c,d). During this exercise, at least one hand should be touching the ground at all times. Improvise with your partner by moving around him and reacting to his movements, not by blocking his moves but rather by going around him and entangling him in a web of movements. When you see an opening or a hole, try to go through it by passing between his legs or under his body as if it were a bridge. When your partner tries to go under you, let him do it by creating holes through which he can pass. Do not use the *negativa*.[23]

In this exercise you should improvise and try to be creative.

This exercise, as well as the "movement improvisation (standing up)," are basic if you intend to be a creative player who really understands and is at one with the spirit of capoeira. You should do these exercises in a playful and relaxed state of mind, similar to what we observe when children play games on their own . This means you are playful and having fun but also completely concentrated on what you are doing and what is happening in the game.

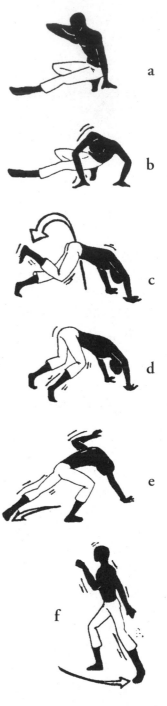

a

b

c

d

e

f

---

23. We do not use the *negativa* in this exercise, nor do we use the *ginga* in the exercise titled "movement improvisation (standing up)," so that the beginner will be forced to improvise and avoid mechanical repetition, which would occur if we were to use the *ginga* or the *negativa*.

3. THE AÚ

(pronounced "Ah-ooo")

The *aú* is known in English as the cartwheel. Through the *aú* the beginner learns how to find his balance while in motion upside-down.

Many beginners are concerned merely with learning fighting techniques, and in this context the *aú* may appear absurd. The beginner should avoid this frame of mind because soon you will learn the tremendously important role which the *aú* plays in the game of capoeira.

The *aú* is also part of the web of unexpected movements which encircles your opponent and leaves him dizzy, making him hesitate, lose his center of balance, and even open his guard. Learning to use the *aú* appropriately is one of the first steps in making the beginner comfortable in awkward situations that often arise in real-life fights, as when you suddenly slip, are thrown in the air or begin tumbling.

The *aú* can be an extremely effective way of approaching an opponent, or fleeing under certain circumstances. The *aú* and upside-down movements in general make the capoeirista very unpredictable, for it enlarges your spectrum of movement possibilities. The *aú* and upside-down movements also help the player understand that capoeira, and life, are not simply a matter of winning and losing; and that if life has many battles and struggles, you also need to learn how to dance, be poetic, have fun, be unpredictable (not always rational and objective), and be slightly crazy and chaotic, if you are to savor the best of life and capoeira.

In diagram a) we see an open aú, usually associated with capoeira *Regional.* In diagram b) we see a closed *aú,* the type usually associated with capoeira *Angola.*

As time goes by, the beginner will begin to master the *aú* in all of its innumerable variations, such as the *aú* with *rolê,* or the *aú coberto,* etc.

Eventually the player will feel as comfortable attacking and dodging while standing upside-down as he does standing right-side-up or close to the floor.

Exercises:

a) Try to do an *aú* to one side and then to another side. At first you will have trouble going to your weak side. Try to work through this, because a *capoeirista* should always be adept at going to either side. If you have trouble, try a very closed *aú* (i.e., with legs bent). It can even start off as a little hop, with both hands touching the ground for support; slowly your *aú* will begin opening up.

b) Practice the *aú*. This time be very careful not to look at the floor, but rather to fix your gaze on a person who is in front of you.

c) Practice the *aú* in between the basic *ginga* movement and movement improvisation exercises (on the floor and standing up). Eventually try to incorporate the *aú* into these movements so that one flows smoothly into the next.

d) Practice the *aú* with a partner using the basic *ginga* as well as the movement improvisation exercises (on the floor and standing up).

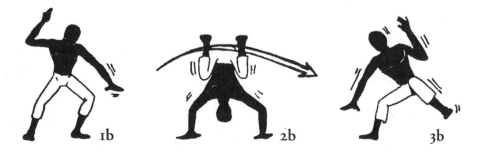

DEFENSIVE MOVEMENTS

During the first three sessions the pupil has begun to learn the basic forms of movement. Let us now begin to explore defensive movements. In capoeira, the idea is not to block kicks but to avoid them altogether. Actually, the pupil has already been introduced to one defensive movement, since the *negativa* and the *rolê* (basic elements of the ground game) can be used as defensive movements.

In an actual game each situation is unique, so the capoeirista must adapt each attack, escape, dodge, counterattack or takedown according to the circumstance that presents itself.

This ability to react intuitively according to the situation at hand is one of the most difficult to master. It is, however, a prerequisite to being able to achieve a good level of play. As mere beginners, we will limit ourselves for the time being to learning some classic defensive movements, and to incorporating these into the movements we have already learned. Later on we will understand how these exercises were the first steps in helping one to react intuitively to the situation at hand.

Eventually, though, you will see that while capoeira has some very efficient kicks for attacking an opponent, it becomes even more dangerous when the player is adept at using the defensive movements to move under an opponent's kick and then take him down, or to prepare for a counterattack for which there is no defense.

1. THE COCORINHA

If he is attacked by a horizontal blow (like a slap), the capoeirista dodges it by going into the *cocorinha,* with the weight evenly distributed on both feet. One of the hands protects the head, while the other can touch the ground lightly. This is typical of the traditional capoeira *Regional.* Many times, as a player drops into the *cocorinha,* he gives a small hop forward, trying to come in under the kick so that he may get close to his adversary.

Exercises:

a) Do the basic *ginga* in front of a chair, and go into the *cocorinha* by taking a small hop forward. After going down, stand up and continue to *ginga*.

b) In front of a chair, do the movement improvisation (standing up) and incorporate the *cocorinha*.

c) Repeat the above exercise, this time with a partner; execute the *cocorinha* when you believe that the opponent is in a position to be able to attack with a circular kick or horizontal blow. The *cocorinha* is not suitable to avoid direct and straightforward kicks. (Note: There should be no kicks or blows for the time being.)

2. RESISTÊNCIA

The *resistência* is similar to the *cocorinha,* only in this case the weight is distributed unevenly between the feet, and the torso leans a little to one side; there is no forward hop, since the *resistência* is exe-

cuted when the opponent is already very close. As you will see later, the *resistência* can be the first step in taking down your opponent when he throws a direct kick.[24] The *resistência* teaches you to move to the side from the line of attack without retreating.

Exercises:

Similar to *cocorinha*.

3. QUEDA DE QUATRO

Unlike the *cocorinha* (where the capoeirista attempts to come in

under the kick), in the *queda de quatro* the player dodges, moving away his torso and

---

24. The resistência can lead directly to take-downs such as the *cruz* or the *rasteira*.

72

face while keeping his feet in the same location. From this position the capoeirista usually stretches out one of his legs and moves into a *negativa,* and then executes a *rolê* (in order to move in or away as dictated by the circumstances). Typical of *Capoeira Angola.*

Exercises:

Similar to *cocorinha.*

4. ESQUIVA

This is a very intuitive and organic way of dodging a horizontal blow, which consists of simply taking the head and torso out of the trajectory of attack.

Exercises:

Similar to *cocorinha.*

THE BASIC KICKS

A fter having completed the three sessions devoted to movement, and one to defense, we finally come to the fifth session where we explore kicks.

"Finally!" says the beginner. "Now I can learn how to kick some ass."

This euphoria, though, often turns into disappointment, since the first kicks are often done awkwardly and lack power. This is normal. Before you know it, though, you will have mastered these basic kicks.

Training sessions should from now on be done in the following sequence:

1) Initial warm-up—We haven't talked about this yet, but a warm-up session is a good idea before you begin your capoeira training. If you can do a warm-up using *ginga,* movement improvisation and a bit of stretching, that would be suitable. If you don't know what I am talking about, just run around and move for five to ten minutes.

2) Movement improvisation standing up (exercise c) of *ginga*)

3) Movement improvisation on the floor (exercise i) of *negativa* and *rolê*)

4) Practice kicks for one and two players. (Do only one type of kick per practice session for now.)

If the beginner does not have a partner for the exercises, he should do the exercises for one person only. With each new training session he will incorporate a new kick.

1. MEIA LUA DE FRENTE

In this kick, the outstretched leg moves in the form of an arc and then returns to its initial position. It is as if you were to pass an outstretched leg over a chair.

In the diagram we can see the execution of the kick from a lateral profile.

Exercises:

a) Practice the kick according to the diagram, passing your leg over a chair placed directly in front of you (ten times each leg).

b) *Ginga* in front of a chair, but this time you should be about five feet back. From the *ginga* position, take one step forward with your back leg and then kick with the front leg. Your foot should pass

1

74

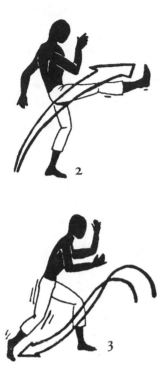

over the chair. The kicking leg should be back when it comes down. Now continue the *ginga* movement and repeat with the other leg (ten times each leg).

c) *Ginga* accompanying the *ginga* of your partner (as if your partner were your reflection in a mirror); step in with your rear leg, and with the front leg execute the *meia lua de frente.* Your partner should avoid the kick by going down into the *cocorinha,* using a small hop so that he will end very close to your support leg. This exercise should begin slowly, with the person who is kicking warning his partner that the kick is about to come (ten times each leg). Later the exercise can be done faster without any warnings (when I say later I mean in a month's time, provided you are taking class or practicing three times a week). See drawings of Bimba's First Sequence in order to understand the kick (*meia lua de frente*) and defensive movement (*cocorinha*).

d) Later (in three months' time), the two partners will do the movement improvisation (standing up) and one of the partners will attack with the *meia lua de frente* without warning. His partner will avoid the blow using one of the defensive movements that we have already seen (*cocorinha, resistência, queda de quatro, negativa*), or by simply taking his head and body out of the line of attack by going under the kick.

2. ARMADA
(Armada Girando)

This is a kick that will take some getting used to for the beginner. The player steps across with his left foot (1); he spins his head and torso first until he is able to see the target (the head has spun about

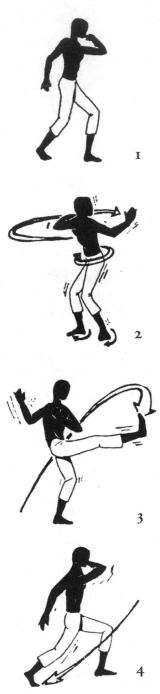

180 degrees at this point), and then there is a corresponding spin from the feet (2). Only then is the kick released (3). It's as if the torso had "pulled" the leg like a spring.

Exercises:

a) Practice the kick according to the diagram (ten times each leg).

b) Practice the kick using the outstretched hand of a partner as a target. (Note: The person with the outstretched hand should place the target at the level of the abdomen. As time goes by, he will raise the target until it corresponds to the height of a person).

c) Do the basic *ginga* in front of someone who has his hands outstretched as a target; take one step forward so that you will be in a position to release the armada; execute the kick ten times each leg.

d) Two persons *ginga* accompanying each other's pace: one of them takes a step forward and attacks with an *armada*; the other person goes down into the *cocorinha* or *resistência* (ten times each leg); see drawings in Bimba's Seventh Sequence.

e) Three months after starting the training sessions, do the movement improvisation (standing up). Execute the *armada* without warning. Your partner should dodge it intuitively by going under the movement or by using one of the defensive movements shown before. The important thing is to avoid the blow (as opposed to blocking it) by using a classical capoeira defense movement or by using an intuitive defense movement.

Note: This sort of exercise, which is linked to the movement improvisation exercises and meant to be done three months after beginning, is of basic importance in this method. If you have read and thought about the different training steps in the *Ginga* section, you will understand that this is one more step toward a creative style of playing capoeira.

3. QUEIXADA
(pronounced "kay-shah-da")

The *queixada* is like the inverse of a *meia lua de frente*. It can be done in two ways: The player twists his torso, which is then used to "pull" the front leg, (sequence a); or, the leg is thrust forward, and thus the kick is accomplished with a small twist of the torso (sequence b).

Which kick you choose depends on the relative position between the two players. The basic difference is that one kick uses the back leg and the other uses the front leg. This kick should be directed at the side of the opponent's head, or at the opponent's cheek (*queixo* in Portuguese).

Exercises:

a) Execute the kick according to the diagrams.

b) Practice the kick using your partner's hand as a target (ten times each leg).

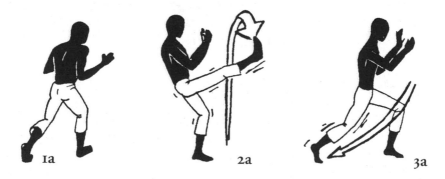

1a   2a   3a

1b   2b   3b

c) Take a step forward before executing the kick (five times each leg).

d) Do the basic *ginga* using a partner's outstretched hand as a target; take a step forward before executing the kick (five times each leg).

e) Two people *ginga* facing each other; one partner takes a step forward and executes the *queixada* (sequence a); the other training partner takes a small hop forward (which will place him close to the support leg of the person kicking) as he goes down into the *cocorinha;* he gets up when the kick passes over him and continues to *ginga* (five times each leg).

f) The two partners *ginga;* one steps forward and executes the *queixada* (sequence a), and the other intuitively dodges the kick. Take note that there is a correct side that you should go down on in order to avoid the blow (five times each).

g) Later on (after three months): Do the movement improvisation (standing up) exercise and use the *queixada* unexpectedly on your partner, who will in turn try to avoid the kick as best he can. You will execute the *queixada* twice (one kick with each leg) and then it will be your partner's turn to attack.

4. MARTELO-DO-CHÃO

This is a kick that is released from the *negativa* position. Frequently used as a means of attack from the floor against someone who is standing, it is more typical of *Capoeira Angola.*

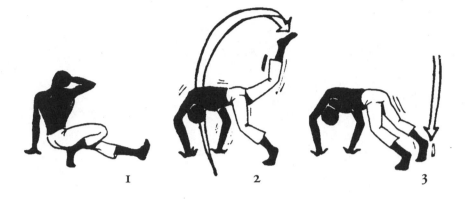

1   2   3

Exercises:

a) *Ginga,* go down into a *negativa,* execute the *martelo-de-chão,* stand up, continue to *ginga* (ten times with each leg).

b) *Ginga* somewhat at a distance from your target (i.e., your partner's hand), go down into a *negativa,* approach the target and execute the kick (ten times each leg).

c) Three months later: Do the movement improvisation (on the floor) exercise, and without warning execute a *martelo-do-chão.* Your partner will avoid it as best he can by getting out of the kick's trajectory.

5. CHAPA-DE-COSTAS

The *chapa-de-costa* is typical of *Capoeira Angola.* The kick usually begins with the *negativa;* then the player approaches his opponent in the *rolê;* then he aims for the opponent's face or groin area with the *chapa.* The *chapa-de-costa* is similar to a mule kick, and when it is done with both legs at the same time it is called a "double mule kick."

Exercises:

Do the movement improvisation (on the floor) using the *martelo-do-chão* and the *chapa-de-costas* as a means of attack. You will execute two kicks; then it is your partner's turn to execute two kicks.

1   2   3

Note: With the *chapa-de-costas* we finish our ninth exercise. We have already learned elements of defense and attack. The attack movements can be separated into those executed standing up (i.e., *meia lua de frente, armada, and queixada)* and those executed from the floor (i.e., *martelo-do-chão, chapa-de-costas).*

In our tenth training session we train the kick we feel is our weakest.

6. BENÇÃO
(Chapa-de-frente)

1

2

The *benção* is the movement shown in the diagrams (2, 3 and 4). Normally, the capoeirista takes a step forward from the ginga, in the direction of the opponent, and then releases the kick. (Sequences 1 and 2 show this movement.) The *benção* is an especially effective kick when it catches the opponent in full.

Many times the *benção* is thrown with a lot of violence; the initial step is transformed into an actual leap, and the entire weight of the player is used in the kick. In this case (this *benção* is called the *benção pulada*) the person throwing the kick will not have the control to be able to recoil the kick after it is thrown. If you miss the target, the tendency

is to fall forward. Herein lies a lesson: In capoeira, when you attack in a very violent manner you are usually exposed to a counterattack if the kick is not effective. Usually, kicks that "go for broke" are a two-edged sword, not only dangerous for the person being attacked but also for the attacker himself.

Exercises:

a) Execute the *benção* (diagrams 2 and 5) standing still (ten times each leg). Notice that you are not really kicking the opponent but "pushing" him.

b) *Ginga.* Take a step forward and execute the *benção* (diagrams 1 to 5) (ten times each leg).

c) Practice the leaping *benção* against a punching bag of the type used by boxers, if one is available (ten times each leg).

The *benção* shown here is more typical of the *Capoeira Regional.* The *Angoleiro* releases the kick but does not recoil his leg and finish standing (as in diagram 5); instead, from position 4 he goes right down into a *negativa.*

7. MARTELO-EM-PÉ

A quick and explosive kick. The *martelo* is traditionally done using the top of the foot, but many young capoeira players have adapted techniques from different Eastern martial arts. Observe the movement of the arms (diagram 2), which helps to add explosion to the

kick and to assure that the kicker does not lose his balance. The foot kicks, and comes back quickly and under control. In the drawing we can see the player is stepping into the kick from the *ginga*.

1   2   3

Exercises:

a) Do the exercise according to the diagrams (ten times each leg). Do not go for quickness or explosion in the first exercises using the *martelo;* try to do the movement correctly at first, and the quickness and power will come with time (which could mean months or even years).

b) *Ginga* in front of a training partner with an outstretched hand, take one step forward and execute the *martelo* against the extended hand (ten times each leg). Note: Adjust until you find the right distance. Your foot should touch the hand when your leg is fully extended. The outstretched hand should first be held about waist-high and, as time goes by, the hand can be raised to head-level (this will happen months later for beginners).

1a 2a 3a

8. MEIA LUA DE COMPASSO

(Rabo-de-arraia)

4a

Along with the *rasteira* (which we will learn when we explore takedowns), the *meia lua de compasso* is one of the trademarks of capoeira. It is also one of the most efficient and deadly kicks. The kick is done with the heel (see diagram 3).

The beginner will execute the kick so awkwardly that it will be hard to believe that soon the kick will be fast and powerful. The *meia lua* usually begins from the standing *ginga* position (diagram 1a), however, it can also be used effectively starting from the *negativa* on the floor (see sequence b). An important detail is the position of the hands on the floor before executing the kick, as seen in diagram 3 of sequence b. The relative position between the person who is executing the kick and the target can be seen further on, in Bimba's Sixth Sequence.

Exercises:

a) Execute the *meia lua de compasso* as shown in the diagrams for sequence a) (ten times each leg).

b) Approach your target (the extended hand of your partner) as you *ginga* and release the kick (ten times each leg); note that the person executing the kick looks at the target in between his legs

(position 2a)—beginners often commit the mistake of looking at the floor when they execute the *meia lua de compasso.*

c) One month later: Both players *ginga,* one of the players warns that he is going to attack and then releases the *meia lua de compasso,* the other one dodges the kick intuitively (ten times each leg).

d) Three month later: Do the movement improvisation (standing up) exercise and without warning execute the *meia lua de compasso.* You will execute the kick, do some more improvisation and attack again. Then your partner will attack twice in the same manner. Defend yourself intuitively.

We've now arrived at the fourteenth training session, and have finished the basic kicks. In the last four sessions, the beginner has already begun to incorporate parts of the *jogo,* or game of capoeira, into his training session. If you are self-taught, that is, training alone or with a friend according to the method recommended in this book, the time has arrived to come out of your shell and get to know other capoeiristas who are more advanced (if you have not done so already). The time has also arrived to purchase your own *berimbau* and to become acquainted with it, first in an informal manner and later by learning the traditional rhythms used in capoeira games.

The beginner should direct himself to a local capoeira academy. As the saying goes, though: *"Pisando em terras alheias, pisar no chão devagar."* ("When walking in foreign lands, watch your step.") Limit yourself to watching the class at first. One can learn a lot by simply observing. Don't play with people you don't know, as a matter of fact, for the time being; don't even play with friends who are more advanced than you: *"Quem não pode com mandinga não carrega patúa."*

The decision whether to continue to learn alone or to join an instructor is yours to make. Follow your intuition. But as we observed before, the final objective of the capoeirista is the *jogo,* in the *roda,* to the sound of the *berimbau,* with other capoeiristas. Keep this in mind and before long, without even noticing it, you will feel perfectly at ease in the middle of the *roda,* playing capoeira.

BIMBA'S SEQUENCES

As I mentioned earlier, each teacher has his own teaching method. Nonetheless, ever since capoeira began to be institutionalized (in the 1930s) and began to be taught formally in academies, the use of prearranged sequences as a teaching tool has been common among many instructors. Unfortunately, it is now impossible to learn capoeira intuitively and as part of a cultural whole, as you could in Salvador up until about thirty or forty years ago. The times have changed, and Brazilian society has been undergoing enormous convulsions as it tries to enter the twenty-first century and to modernize its economy to keep up with the rest of the world.

Like everything else, capoeira has been touched by the changes surrounding it—and it could not be otherwise. In fact, capoeira is a school for life. It reflects life and the environment that surrounds it as if it were a mirror, as if it were a microcosm where the capoeirista can learn how to deal with life in a very special way.

One inevitable change, as capoeira has spread throughout Brazil and the world, is that the teaching of capoeira has become more structured. There are obvious reasons for this: Class enrollments have swelled, and teachers can no longer give the individual attention to students that they would like. Also, today's students often cannot dedicate entire days to the study of capoeira; rather, they often fit classes into very busy schedules, so they must get the most out of the short time they spend in class.

By giving the students rote exercises to practice, the teacher needs only explain the exercise once, and the students can then work together on that exercise. Also, it cannot be denied that practice makes perfect and that practicing a sequence over and over can produce impressive results.

There are, however, dangers with this approach. Many masters today, including myself, are alarmed at a tendency toward mechanical and predictable movements. This is totally contrary to the spirit of capoeira, which in its essence should be improvised and unpredictable.

In spite of all these changes, capoeira has survived and prospered, and remains an art whose "goal is inconceivable even to the wisest of capoeiristas," in the words of the venerable Mestre Pastinha. It is thus up to students and teachers alike to try to combat the forces that want to standardize capoeira, keeping in mind that the sequences themselves are not the problem; the problem lies in showing a blind subservience to these effective teaching tools. This can be done by creating exercises and methods that stress creativity and improvisation, as we are attempting to do here.

Of all of the structured teaching methods, in my opinion, Mestre Bimba's Eight Sequences (included in their entirety in this chapter) are still without a doubt one of the best ways of learning *Capoeira Regional.*

The sequences should be done from the basic *ginga* at a fast rhythm (the rhythm of *São Bento Grande Regional,* for example), although initially they should be practiced at a slower rhythm until beginners master the moves and can execute them without hesitating.

You should move on to a new sequence as soon as you have memorized the previous one, even though all of the kicks may not have been perfected yet. It will take approximately ten to fifteen sessions before you can complete all Eight Sequences smoothly.

The training sessions should be structured as follows from now on:

a) Warm-up;

b) Movement improvisation exercises, standing up and on the floor;

c) Exercises involving kicks: *Ginga* facing your partner, in synch with his movements; warn him that you are about to attack ("Now!") and your partner will then avoid the blow by dodging it. Do this with both legs, then trade positions with him (ten times each leg). Practice only one type of kick each session (i.e., *meia lua de frente, meia lua de compasso, armada* or *queixada*).

FIRST SEQUENCE

(In the diagram, we see the two players—"Plain" on the left and "Striped" on the right.)

Plain: *Meia lua de frente, meia lua de frente, armada* and *aú.*

Striped: *Cocorinha, cocorinha* and *negativa.*

1) The two players begin by executing the basic *ginga.* They accompany each other's pace.

2) Plain takes one step forward (left foot) in Striped's direction, situating himself so that he will be able to attack .

Note: At first Plain should warn Striped of the moment of attack.

3) Plain attacks Striped with a *meia lua de frente* (right foot) while Striped defends by going into a *cocorinha* (by taking a forward hop and going into a crouch near Plain's support leg).

4) Just as soon as Plain's right leg finishes passing over Striped's head, Striped stands up.

4

5) Immediately Plain attacks with another *meia lua de frente,* this time with the left leg. Striped goes down into the *cocorinha* again, placing himself near Plain's support leg.

5

6) Plain finishes the *meia lua de frente* (left leg), but instead of placing the left foot back to its initial position, as would be expected, Plain ends the kick by dropping his foot forward, thus placing himself in a position to add an *armada,* which will surely hit Striped when he stands up from the *cocorinha.*

6

7

8

7), 8) & 9) Plain spins his body quickly and releases the *armada,* but Striped does not stand up. Rather, he goes down into a *negativa,* with the left leg stretched and the left foot placed in such a way that it could take Plain down by pulling on his left foot. Plain releases the armada using the right leg. Striped has already begun to prepare himself to come out of the *negativa* so that he can catch Plain when he escapes in an *aú.*

9

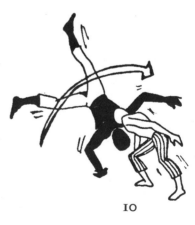

10) Plain escapes by doing an *aú* to his left. Striped changes sides on the *negativa* and approaches Plain, trying to give him a head-butt to the chest. Note: Come as close to your opponent as possible without knocking him over.

10

SECOND SEQUENCE

Plain: Two *martelos, cocorinha, benção* and *aú.*
Striped: Two *bandas, armada, negativa* and head-butt.

1) Plain and striped *ginga* facing each other, and accompany each other's pace. Striped notices that Plain is going to attack him with a *martelo.*

2) Plain steps forward and to the outside in an attempt to set up his *martelo.* Striped, however, anticipates his movement and attempts to take him down with a *banda* (a standing sweep, which will be explained in the section of the book devoted to takedowns). Plain releases his *martelo,* but does not find his target. Striped's foot is set behind Plain's support leg, ready to sweep; however, he refrains from taking him down.

3) Plain completes the *martelo* with the right leg, and after returning to the ground with his right foot, quickly goes into a *martelo* with his left foot. Striped again anticipates his movement, and again positions himself for the *banda,* where he could easily take Plain down.

4) Striped takes his right foot out, and quickly turns his body to go into an *armada*. Plain has already finished his left *martelo,* and is in a position to defend himself.

5) Striped releases the left *armada,* but Plain dodges the kick by going into a *cocorinha.*

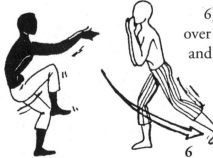

6) Striped's *armada* has just passed over Plain's head when Plain stands up and goes into a *benção.*

7) Plain executes the *benção* with his right leg, and Striped goes down into the *negativa* (right leg outstretched), trying to set his right foot behind Plain's support leg.

7

8) Plain recoils his *benção* and prepares to go into an *aú*. Striped prepares to go into a *rolê*, which will position him for a head-butt.

8

9) Plain executes the *aú*, while Striped comes in for the head butt.

9

THIRD SEQUENCE

Plain: *Queixada, queixada, cocorinha, benção* and *aú.*
Striped: *Cocorinha, cocorinha, armada, negativa, rolê* and *cabeçada.*

1) Both players *ginga.* Plain arrives at the point in his *ginga* where he would normally pull the right leg back.

2) Instead, he steps forward with his right leg.

3) Plain attacks with a right *queixada.* Striped, however, avoids the kick by falling into the *cocorinha.*

4) The kick passes over Striped, who then stands up, already inside of Plain's guard. In a game, Striped would have the clear advantage at this point.

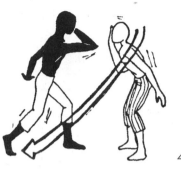

4

5) Plain recovers and immediately attacks with another *queixada,* this time using his left leg to kick. Striped again takes a small hop forward while going down into the *cocorinha,* thus putting himself near Plain's support leg.

5

6) Plain finishes the second *queixada* in the position shown in the drawing. Striped stands up from the *cocorinha,* already in a position to counterattack with an *armada.*

6

7

8

7) Striped spins his body quickly and releases a right *armada*. Plain, however, has already gone down into the *cocorinha*, thus evading Striped's *armada*.

9

8) Plain stands up from the *cocorinha* ready to execute the *benção*. Striped, however, has already finished the *armada* and quickly goes into a *negativa*.

9) Plain would suffer an ugly fall were Striped to pull his support leg.

10) Plain escapes with an *aú* to his left. Striped responds by trying a *cabeçada*.

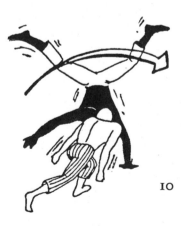

10

FOURTH SEQUENCE

Plain: *Galopante, negativa* and *rolê*.
Striped: *Arrastão* and *aú*.

1) Plain and Striped *ginga*. In this sequence we will encounter some moves that we have not yet covered: the *galopante* (an open-handed blow that targets the opponent's ear) and the *arrastão* (which we will review in the takedown section).

2) Plain steps forward and attacks with a right-handed *galopante*. Striped steps in with the right foot, and strikes his shoulder against Plain's hip while pulling him from behind the knees, thus knocking him down.

3) Plain falls to the ground, and Striped pulls the right foot in.

4) Plain was able to fall in the *nega-tiva* position, but Striped is already getting ready to escape into an *aú*.

5) Plain uses the *rolê* in order to follow Striped and strike him with a headbutt.

FIFTH SEQUENCE

Plain: *Giro, joelhada* and *aú.*
Striped: *Arpão de cabeça, negativa* and
cabeçada.

1) Both players *ginga* accompanying
each other.

2) Plain spins on his heels (*giro*),
threatening to throw a kick. Striped reacts
by going down into a *cocorinha,* since he
is anticipating an *armada* that is never
released. He then goes into an *arpão-de-
cabeça:* a violent move using the body's
entire forward momentum to deliver a
head-butt to the abdomen of the opponent. Striped places both arms in front
of his face in order to protect it in case of
a counterattack, while delivering the head-
butt.

3) Plain releases a *joelhada* (a knee
blow) aimed at Striped's face. Striped
retreats into a *negativa* without having
completed the *cabeçada.*

4) & 5) Plain prepares to escape with an *aú*. Striped should follow Plain in a *rolê* so that he can strike him with a head-butt.

4

5

SIXTH SEQUENCE

Plain: *Meia lua de compasso* and *cocorinha*.
Striped: *Cocorinha* and *meia lua de compasso*.

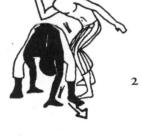

1) Both players *ginga* at the same pace.
Plain prepares to go into a *meia lua*.

2) Plain steps in with his left foot in
order to set up a *meia lua de compasso*
with his right foot.

3) Plain executes the *meia lua* and
Striped defends by going into the *cocor-inha*.

4) Plain finishes the kick. Striped, from the *cocorinha,* has already taken a step forward with his right foot in order to set up a counterattack with the left leg in a *meia lua de compasso.*

4

5) Striped executes the counterattack with the left leg, and Plain goes down into a *cocorinha.*

5

SEVENTH SEQUENCE

Plain: *Armada, cocorinha, benção* and *aú*.
Striped: *Cocorinha, armada* and *negativa*.

1) The diagram shows the training partners already in full swing: From the *ginga*, Plain took a step forward with his left foot and is ready to release a right-footed *armada*. Striped responds by going down into a *cocorinha*.

2) Striped stands up while simultaneously stepping in with his right foot in order to release a left-footed *armada*. Plain has not yet completed his kick when Striped begins his counterattack.

3) Striped releases his counterattack, a left *armada*. Plain had already completed his kick quickly, and entered into a *cocorinha*.

4) Plain stands up with a *benção,* and Striped places his outstretched foot in the *negativa* position behind Plain's support leg to prepare for a sweep.

4

5) Plain prepares to escape in an *aú.* Striped changes legs in the *negativa,* and approaches to deliver a head-butt. Plain escapes in an *aú.*

5

EIGHTH SEQUENCE

Plain: *Benção* and *aú*.
Striped: *Negativa, rolê* and *cabeçada*.

1) Both partners *ginga* at the same pace. Plain steps in quickly with a *benção*. Striped goes down into a *negativa*.

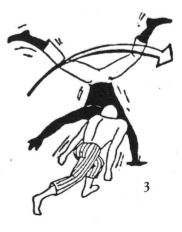

2) Plain executes the *benção*. Striped, while in the *negativa*, has already placed his front foot behind Plain's support leg.

3) Plain escapes in an *aú*, while Striped uses the *rolê* to come in and execute a *cabeçada*.

Note: Always execute the Eighth Sequence at a fast pace *(São Bento Grande de Regional)*.

Do all exercises using first one foot and then the other.

CINTURA DESPREZADA

The *cintura desprezada* is a sequence of four acrobatic exercises created by Mestre Bimba, wherein the capoeirista learns to always fall on his feet. As the name indicates (*cintura desprezada* means "scorned hip"), the old master felt that not enough attention was paid to the *"jogo de cintura,"* or hip movement.

a

a*

b

b*

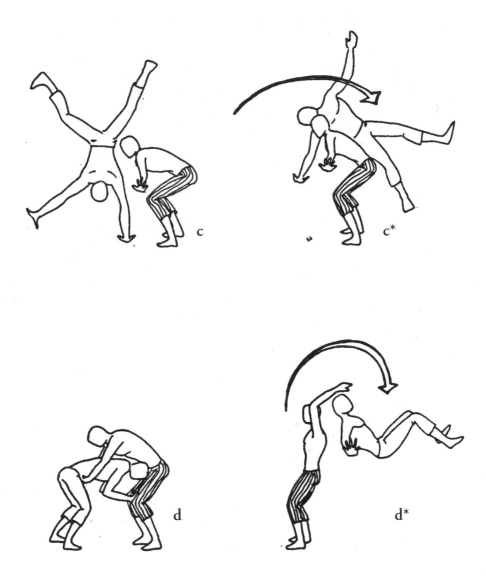

c

c*

d

d*

It must be stressed that these exercises should be done only under the supervision of an experienced teacher, so as to avoid injuries. Also, we must note that the person who is throwing his partner has an important role to play in helping make sure that his partner lands properly.

TAKEDOWNS

The beginner already has a sufficient amount of moves and kicks in order to be able to develop his game. Nonetheless, there are times when, in spite of a lot of hard work, the student does not see any progress—many times it even seems that the student is "unlearning." It is normal in capoeira (once the basic learning phase is over) for progress to come in spurts. You will go for months without seeing any apparent progress, and suddenly, when you least expect it, you jump to a new level in your game.

Nonetheless, you still have to be introduced to the most subtle, the most refined, the most efficient and without a doubt the most dangerous (for the opponent, of course) part of the game: takedowns.

The good capoeirista can play the game both standing up and on the ground; he knows how to play *Regional* and *Angola;* he composes songs, plays the *berimbau,* the *pandeiro* and the *atabaque.* He knows the history, the philosophy and the ritual of capoeira.

The exceptional capoeirista does that and much more: He is an expert in taking his opponent down; he knows and has mastered the secrets of the *rasteira,* the many types of *bandas,* the *tesoura* and the *entradas.* He takes literally the popular proverb that says: "The harder they come, the harder they fall."

As a matter of fact, I start to teach and practice the takedowns only about six months (or even a year) after the beginner has started to learn capoeira. I do not teach them one a day, as we have been doing with the basic kicks and with the sequences, but spend one or two weeks practicing a single takedown before moving on to the next one. Takedowns require a new and higher level of understanding of capoeira, and the learning process should be slow enough that the student can savor this new insight.

1. RASTEIRA

Along with the *meia lua de compasso,* this sweep is one of capoeira's trademark movements. When you understand the *rasteira* you are very close to understanding the phi-losophy behind the art form known as capoeira. Whoever has mastered its movement and knows how to exe-cute it within the fraction of a sec-ond when he is attacked, will know how to overcome the most violent and aggressive opponent.

The *rasteira* represents the victory of knowledge over brute force, of shrewdness over strength. It is the weapon of the weak against the strong, of the oppressed against the oppressor.

As with all of the takedowns, the *rasteira* is executed by the capoeirista when he is attacked. Therein lies the difficulty in mastering the art of the takedown: In the heat of the game, the capoeirista is attacked quickly and violently, and there is no time to think or hesitate. Intuitively, he goes into the *rasteira,* simultaneously dodg-ing the attack and pulling the sup-port leg of the aggressor.

The fall is not pretty. Usually, when the *rasteira* is well-executed, the attacker falls on his back and—if he is not a capoeirista—it is not unusual for the back of his head to hit the floor, which can be very dangerous indeed.[25] By doing the following exercises, the beginner will learn to do the *rasteira* instinctively.

Exercises:

a) Practice the movement as shown in the diagram (ten times each leg);

b) Execute the *rasteira* from the basic *ginga* (ten times each leg);

c) Both players *ginga,* one attacking with the *benção* and the other defending and counterattacking with the *rasteira* (ten times each leg); in this exercise the person who is doing the takedowns should only go down into the *rasteira* and place the foot. If you were to pull each time, your partner's shin would never be able to withstand it. Toward the end of the training session, try pulling the *rasteira* two or three times just to see if it is working.

---

25. The way to avoid this, if you fall with your back to the floor, is to tuck your chin into your chest.

2. BANDA
(Banda de frente, Rasteira em pé)

We have already seen the *banda de frente* in Bimba's Second Sequence. The *banda* is frequently used against the *martelo* or similar direct kicks. It can also be applied when the opponent is not attacking, as long as the opponent has most of his weight on the leg to which you apply the *banda*. This type of *banda*, however, is rarely successful.

After having set your foot behind the opponent's support leg you usually twist your body to generate torque so as to sweep that foot off the ground. This is sometimes known as a *rasteira em pé*.

Exercises:

a) *Ginga* in front of a person who is standing, and step into the *banda* without completing the sweep (ten times each leg).

b) Repeat above exercise, this time executing the sweep. It may be advisable to use a shin guard for this exercise, although in a well-executed *banda* there should be no contact between the shins—the opponent's foot is simply swept out from under him.

c) Both partners *ginga,* one attacking with a *martelo* and the other reacting with the *banda*. At first, the person who is executing the *martelo* will announce that he is about to kick, but after a few sessions the martelo should be executed without any warning. Only try to take him down during the last few kicks (twenty times each leg).

I

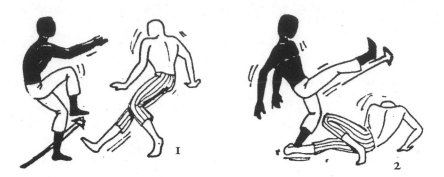

3. NEGATIVA DERRUBANDO

Our old acquaintance the *negativa* can be used not only as a means of movement on the floor but also in a takedown. A good example of this can be seen in the last movements of some of Bimba's Sequences (Third, Seventh and Eighth) where we see one partner attack with a *benção* and the other respond by going into a *negativa* and setting his foot behind the heel of the support leg of the attacker (notice that as Striped goes into a *negativa,* he conveniently dodges Plain's kick).

From that position, the person on the ground would pull his foot and leg in (as we saw when studying the *negativa*) and finish in a standing position while his partner falls.

In the diagrams we see the player going into the *negativa derrubando* from the basic *ginga.* In the diagram, Plain's *benção* has been frozen in midair for demonstration purposes. However, it should never be hanging in the air as seen in the diagram, but should be completed from start to finish as quickly as possible.

Exercises:

a) The best exercises for this takedown are in Bimba's Sequences. Work on trying to be quick enough to position yourself for the sweep while your partner's kicking leg is still in the air. The person kicking should concentrate on completing the kick, and should try to forget that he knows his partner is coming in for the takedown.

4. NEGATIVA WITH A TESOURA

Using forward momentum, the capoeirista goes into a *tesoura* and traps the leg of his opponent. The torque generated by Plain twisting his hip will knock "Striped" down (diagram 3).

Exercises:

a) *Ginga* in front of someone who is standing still in the *ginga* stance; then enter into the *negativa* and trap your opponent's leg with the *tesoura* (ten times each leg).

b) Both partners ginga. One steps into a *benção* while the other steps in with a *negativa tesoura* and traps his opponent's leg (ten times each leg).

1

2

3

5. ARRASTÃO

We already saw this movement in Bimba's Fourth Sequence. The diagram shows in detail the impact of the shoulder against the top of the hip as both hands pull from behind the knee.

This movement is frequently used to defend against a punch or an attack with a club. It is most effective in a game situation when coupled with the element of surprise. It is common for the person who is being taken down to grab at his opponent's back. In that case, the person executing the movement should stand up, forcing his opponent's knees up and causing an ugly fall.

Exercises:

a) Go into the *arrastão* on a person who is stationary (ten times each leg).

b) *Ginga* in front of a stationary person; go into the *arrastão* (ten times each leg).

6. BOCA DE CALÇA

In spite of seeming rather naive, this move works wonderfully when applied quickly and shrewdly. It is very often used by *malandros* at the start of a fight.

In a game situation, when used from the *cocorinha* against a spinning kick (an *armada,* for example), the *boca de calça* is applied against only one leg (the support leg). Note that (as the name, which means pant hem, indicates) the person executing the move grabs the hem of the pants of the person he is trying to knock down.

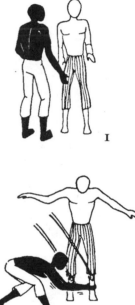

1

Exercises:

Stand in a relaxed and casual manner in front of and close to your partner, who should be standing still. Bend down to grab both pant hems.

2

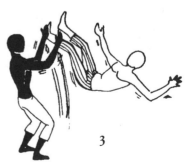

3

7. BOCA-DE-CALÇA DE COSTAS
(Baianada)

A now-classic *malandragem* move used to initiate fights when one has an opponent directly behind him. The diagram shows the *boca de calça* as it is being applied. The capoeirista jumps back at the same time that he bends down to grab the ankles, or the *boca de calça,* of the opponent. The resulting fall is very dangerous.

1

Exercises:

Practice coming in to execute this movement on a training partner who is standing. Beginning from a relaxed and casual position, jump back and reach down quickly and decisively (ten times each leg).

2

3

8. CRUZ

(Cruz de Carreira; Cruz de Encruzilhada)

When you are attacked by a *benção* or a similar kick, you can *esquiva* and take down your opponent with the *cruz*. Depending on the position of the person being attacked, he will *esquiva* to the inside or to the outside; using either of those two *esquivas* the capoeirista can enter and take down the opponent.

It is not easy to learn to come in and execute the *cruz,* but after some practice you will master it.

Exercises:

a) Both players ginga; one does the *benção,* and the other responds with the *cruz* (ten times each leg).

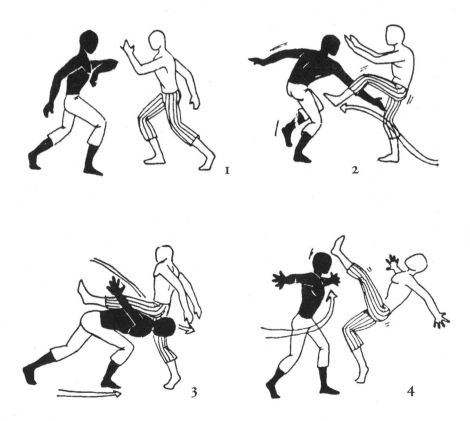

9. BANDA POR DENTRO

This is used if you are attacked by a *martelo* or a similar kick. As we can see in the diagram, the player on the right steps in with his right leg as he prepares to throw a *martelo* with his left leg. The other player astutely anticipates the attack; instead of backing up, he swiftly steps in with his right leg behind his left leg. When he is about to be attacked, he is already in a position to use his left leg to violently pull his opponent's right leg from under him while he pushes him in the chest or the chin (diagram 4).

Exercises:

a) Practice entering into the *banda por dentro* with your partner standing still (ten times).

b) Both partners *ginga*; one enters into a *martelo,* and the other responds with a *banda por dentro* (ten times each leg).

1

2

3

4

10. BANDA DE COSTA

In this takedown, the player thrusts forward, lands on one foot and executes the *banda,* all in one swift movement. It is most effective when both legs of the opponent are swept from under him, but that is quite difficult to do unless your opponent happens to be very naive. This is frequently used against an *armada* or a *queix-ada,* or during an unexpected moment in a game.

Exercises:

a) Step in to execute the *banda* on your partner while he is standing still (ten times each leg).

b) *Ginga* in front of your partner as he stands still, and come in for the *banda de costas* (ten times each leg).

c) Both partners *ginga;* one does a *giro* (spin; see Bimba's Fifth Sequence) while the other comes in to execute the *banda de costa* (ten times each leg).

I

2

11. AÇOITE-DE-BRAÇO

This is a movement geared more towards self-defense in case you are attacked by a person wielding a club or similar weapon, rather than in a game situation.

Exercises:

Execute the *entrada* as shown in the diagrams.

12. TESOURA

(Tesoura-de-costas, Tesoura Furada, Tesoura Voadora)

In the drawing we see that the player who is going to apply the *tesoura* approaches his opponent from afar (drawings 1 and 2). Only when he is near does he actually execute the takedown. The move works because of the torque generated by the body of the attacker, as seen in diagram 4. In practice, the *tesoura* can also be applied much closer.

Exercises:

   a) Come in from afar to execute the *tesoura* (ten times).
   b) Come in from up close (ten times).

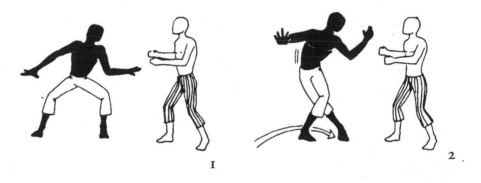

1   2

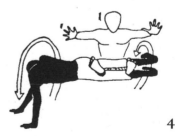

3   4

13. TESOURA-DE-FRENTE

It is common that, in the heat of the moment, as the players are exchanging kicks, one of the players, even for a split-second, foolishly leaves a leg vulnerable for the takedown. If the other player acts swiftly, he will be able to execute the *tesoura de frente.*

Exercises:

a) Execute the *entrada* on your partner as he stands still with one leg forward.

b) *Ginga* in front of your partner as he stands still and executes the *entrada* for the *tesoura-de-frente* (ten times each leg).

1

2

3

14. VINGATIVA

In diagrams 1, 2 and 3 we can see the *vingativa* as it is applied from the floor. Most likely, Striped tried to attack Plain, while Plain was on the floor, with a kick or a *joelhada* (knee-blow). But Plain was able to react quickly and to come up into the *vingativa,* placing his right leg behind his adversary's support leg and completing the takedown by using his leg and torso in a vise-like fashion to make his opponent lose his balance.

This takedown works very efficiently when the person executing it is standing up. In that case, he would proceed from a *ginga* position to the position shown in diagram 2.

1

2

3

Exercises:

a) Come in through the *negativa* on a person who is standing up (ten times each leg).

b) One person *gingas* standing up, and the other plays on the floor, changing directions in the *negativa.* The person standing tries to knee the person who is on the floor, and the latter tries to take down the attacker with a *vingativa* (ten times each side).

c) *Ginga* in front of a person who is standing; come in and execute the *vingativa* (ten times each side).

d) Two partners *ginga.* One executes the *giro,* and the other person comes in and executes the *vingativa* (ten times each side).

15. TOMBO-DE-LADEIRA

Capoeiristas often execute moves that temporarily leave them airborne and thus vulnerable to attack *(S-dobrado, Pulo-do-macaco, or compasso)*. In the *tombo-de-ladeira,* the opponent takes advantage of this split-second, rushes in under the person executing the airborne movement and stands up at the precise moment so as to knock him down. See *Cintura desprezada.*

There you have it: As a beginner, you now have enough material to begin developing your game. Of course, there are other, more advanced exercises for more advanced students, and students can learn some of these when my second and third books are translated into English.

OTHER KICKS AND MOVEMENTS

I want to stress once again the importance of the beginner frequenting the places where capoeira is practiced, even if it is not exactly what one had in mind, because things are rarely as we wish them to be—we sometimes have to learn to deal with what is at hand. Often we see in hindsight that those very critical observations we had once made about a particular place or situation were nothing other than excuses and rationalizations that permitted us to stay within a stagnant comfort zone.

At this point we would like to present you with a few movements now considered classical capoeira movements, well-known among a great number of capoeiristas.

The beginner should continue his training (although it should be remembered that the takedowns presented in the last pages should be practiced only after six months to a year of training), and can explore the following movements according to his curiosity and desire to learn new movements.

1. CHAPA-DE-FRENTE

This is the *Angoleiro's benção*. Let's take this opportunity to explore the differences between the practitioners of *Angola* and *Regional*. Perhaps these differences are attributable to differences in class and education: The *Angoleiro* is the legitimate heir of the marginalized capoeira of the past.

Traditionally, the *Angoleiros* came from the economically least-favored and most-oppressed classes. The *Angoleiro* is accustomed

from a young age to confronting life's blows. The *Regional* practitioner, on the other hand, usually comes from the wealthy class. During his childhood, he usually had the protection of his parents, nannies, good schools, etc., which makes him more daring and to some extent more naive. He is not as accustomed to the hard, face-to-face battles with life and with the social structure. There is always something or someone ready to protect him and give him shelter.

Thus, in *Regional,* when the *benção* is completed and the capoeirista continues to be on his feet, he simply recoils his foot after throwing the kick, without thinking about possible counterattacks. The *Angoleiro,* on the other hand, after completing the *benção* (or in this case *chapa-de-frente*), seeks the protection of the floor against possible takedowns or counterattacks aimed at his face. The *Regional's benção* aims at the chest, and tries to throw the opponent spectacularly out of the *roda*. The *Angoleiro's chapa-de-frente* does not seek such flashy results, but in real-life confrontations it aims for the groin and is very effective.

2. CRUZADO

(Pisão, Escorão)

This is another kick that "goes for broke." It is similar to the *benção pulada* in that if you are successful, great—but if not, you are in trouble. If you miss, and your opponent is quick, he can come in for a take-down, and your resulting fall will not be a pretty sight.

Along with the *martelo* and the *benção,* it is one of the few kicks that can be and should be practiced on a sandbag.

3. S-DOBRADO

(Chapéu-de-Couro, Doublé-S)

This is a movement that is more difficult to describe (through pictures or words) than it is to execute.

The player goes down into a *corta-capim* (diagrams 1 and 2), which is a type of *rasteira,* and at the end of the movement he thrusts

his foot (his left foot, in the drawing) up in the air while he shifts the weight of his body from his right hand to his left hand, and then thrusts his right leg up while supported by his left hand (diagram 4). In diagrams 5 and 6 we see the termination of the movement.

4. CHIBATA

(Rabo-de-Araia)

This is a very fast kick, similar to the *meia lua de compasso*. However, in the *chibata*, you do not put your hand on the ground for support. You make up for this lack of support with the speed with which you execute the kick. This kick is dangerous for the player on the receiving end because of the speed with which it is delivered, and it is dangerous for the person executing it in case he gets swept.

5. PONTEIRA

This is a quick and explosive frontal kick, very common in other martial arts. It uses the ball of the foot to strike the opponent, and leaves you vulnerable to *cruz* and *rasteira*.

6. VÔO-DO-MORCEGO

In the drawings we see the attacker gain momentum and leap into the *Vôo-do-morcego,* with both feet aimed at the face or the solar plexus of the opponent.

This kick can also be applied as a counterattack from the ground while in the *cocorinha* position. In that case, the capoeirista would go down into a *cocorinha* in order to dodge a kick (an *armada,* for example). Once the kick has passed, the player comes up directly from the *cocorinha* position into the position shown in diagram 2, and then extends both feet simultaneously (diagram 3). This kick can be practiced against a sand bag.

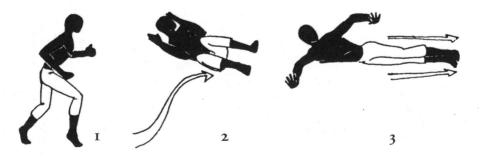

7. MACACO
(Pulo de Macaco)

This can be used as a way of moving within the *roda,* or as a blow when your opponent is behind you during a game.

In the drawings, the person executing the *macaco* changes his support hand, from his right (diagram 2) to his left (diagram 3). But the *macaco* can be executed without this change of hand. In that case, the person in the drawing would execute the *macaco* using the right hand only for support. Usually the kick is executed when the body is more contracted, and it is finalized with a double mule-kick at the end.

8. MEIA LUA PULADA
(Compasso, Meia Lua Solta)

This is a kick commonly used in Rio de Janeiro. The player proceeds as if about to go into a hand-spin (reach for the floor at a

diagonal with your hand going across your body), and completes the kick (diagrams 3 and 4). The kick is delivered with the heel. Some execute this kick without touching the ground with their hand (*meia lua solta*).

The classic counterattack for this movement is the *tombo-de-ladeira*.

9. COMPASSO

Similar to the previous kick; however, the trajectory of the leg follows a vertical plane (whereas, in the previous one, it followed a horizontal plane).

The *compasso* can be executed slowly, under control, in which case it would end in a *negativa* (diagram 4a), or it can be executed violently and with a lot of energy, in which case it would end almost standing up (diagram 4b).

Again, the classic counterattack here is the *tombo-de-ladeira*.

1

2

3

4a

4b

1   2   3

10. CHAPÉU-DE-COURO

The movement begins with a *martelo,* but then proceeds as shown above in diagrams 1, 2 and 3.

1

2

3

11. RABO-DE-ARRAIA

The capoeira terminology varies quite a bit from place to place. The same movement can have two different names, and sometimes the same name describes two different movements.

Among Brazilians, the *rabo-de-arraia* is perhaps the kick most associated with capoeira. Nonetheless, that terms refers to various quite different moves. Depending on the region, *rabo-de-arraia* can also be used to describe the kicks that in this book we call *meia lua de compasso* and *chibata.*

It seems, though, that the original *rabo-de-arraia* is the one shown in the diagram on the left, a movement typical of *Capoeira Angola.*

The kick is executed with the heel, and after completing it the player returns to position (diagram 1). It is not unusual for there to be contact with one heel and then another, as shown in the diagram, or to alternate both legs before returning to the original position (diagram 1).

12. ARMADA WITH MARTELO

The movement begins with an *armada* (diagrams 1, 2 and 3). Halfway through, the person executing this movement, taking advantage of the momentum, jumps while changing legs and goes into a *martelo* (diagram 4).

13. ARPÃO DE CABEÇA

This is a violent head-butt (we already saw this movement in Bimba's Sequences), wherein the person executing it uses the entire weight of his body.

The arms are crossed in front of the player's face in order to protect the face from a *joelhada* (knee-blow). The arms are opened on impact; this increases the power of the movement, which is aimed at the chest or the stomach of the adversary.

14. ESCORUMELO

The *cabeçada* (head-butt) is a move frequently used in capoeira: As long as there is an opening in the defenses, there exists the danger of a *cabeçada*. We have just explored the *arpão-de-cabeça*; here we see a *cabeçada*, which is even more vicious. In this movement the attacker comes up quickly, sliding his head along the chest of the opponent. The point of impact is usually the chin, the nose or the brow. Obviously this movement should never be carried out to completion in a game situation, since the consequences are quite serious.

Although many don't realize it, capoeira also uses many hand blows. In *Angola* they are simply shown; that is, the players don't carry the blows out to completion, but stop just short of contact.[26]

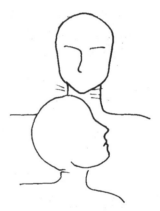

This at times results in a veritable hand ballet of arms, hands and elbows—the so-called *jogo de mão*. In the *Regional*, which pays less attention to ritual and puts more emphasis on fight, the hand blows (the *galopante*, for example) are often carried out to completion.

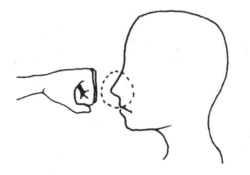

15. ASFIXIANTE

A brisk and direct punch aimed at the nose-mouth region.

---

26. In some of the hand movements in *Angola*, the players pretend to have a *navalha*, or knife.

16. GALOPANTE

A slap with your hand cupped—the entire outstretched arm and torso twist when executing this movement so as to generate more power. It is aimed at the base of the ear. This is also an extremely dangerous movement that can cause damage to the eardrum, and should never be carried out to completion in a *roda*.

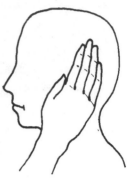

17. GODEME

This is a blow delivered by the knuckles of your fisted hand. A brisk and explosive movement is made with the forearm, and aimed at the brow.

18. CUTELO

Any blow delivered using the outer edge of your stiffened hand.

19. CUTEVELADA

The elbows, due to the very movement of the arms in the *ginga*, are frequently used in capoeira.

20. DEDEIRA

A classic movement: The rigid index and middle fingers are used to poke the eye of the opponent. The element of surprise is key here. Obviously tremendously dangerous, and

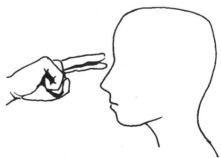

not to be carried out to completion (many times in the *roda* players will merely "show" this movement when there is an opening).

21. TELEFONE

A double slap to both ears simultaneously with hands cupped. Again, very dangerous and not to be carried out to completion in a *roda*.

> Capoeira,
> *Mandinga* of the slave
> yearning to be free.
> Its beginning has no method,
> Its end is inconceivable
> even to the wisest of mestres.
>
> (Mestre Pastinha)

THE LANGUAGE OF ANGOLA

Capoeira Angola possesses its own language, which is often elusive to the non-initiated.

In the section entitled "O Jogo" ("The Game") we described briefly and superficially a situation where one of the players stands with his arms open, and the other player, after several *aús* and demonstrations of his flexibility and control, approaches his opponent, checks one of the legs of the player who is standing in order to prevent an unexpected kick, and slowly rises until they face each other with their arms outstretched and their hands touching. In this position, they take a few steps forward accompanying the rhythm of the beat, stop, and then take a few steps backwards.

This type of dialogue is one of the richest—and as amazing as it might seem, one of the most derided—aspects of *Capoeira Angola*.

135

PASSO-À-DOIS

There are many ways in which the individuals can come together in the *passo-à-dois*. Furthermore, they vary greatly according to the individuals involved and the situations that arise. A lot of *malícia* and a deep knowledge of the basics of the game are needed in order to be able to respond appropriately to whatever situation may arise, the reason being that, although these movements are often very ritualized, at other times they are more improvised and treacherous.

The *passo-à-dois* has different meanings, depending on the level at which one wants to understand it:

- Objectively, it is a way of resting and catching one's breath during the game, or a way of breaking the dynamics of the game of your opponent (as in basketball, when a coach asks for a time-out).

- From a martial-arts perspective, it strengthens the awareness of the player, who is required to approach an opponent from whom he does not know what to expect. Situations preceding actual fights in bars, on the street, etc., many times have this characteristic.

- From a philosophical perspective, the *passo-à-dois* teaches us that when someone is called to interact (in a new job or romance, or even buying or selling a car), that person should go in a very relaxed and self-confident way, but always keep an eye on his opponent to prevent any treachery. We also see that the most dangerous moments in any transaction are when you make the first contact or when you end the transaction and the partners are separating.

All of these levels of knowledge and experience are present in *Angola's* ritualistic movements, but few people really understand what is going on.

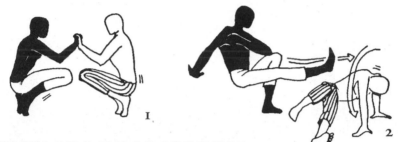

CHAMADA DE COCORINHA

Two players, while in the *cocorinha* position with both hands touching, move sideways with several small hops; one of the players breaks these successive hops with a *chapa de frente*, but the other player, just in the nick of time, manages to escape in the *negativa* and *rolê*.

PASSAGEM DE TESOURAS

In the *passagem de tesouras*, one of the players slides underneath the open legs of his opponent. It is not unusual for the person sliding to attempt to strike his opponent with his heel (a *calcanheira*), or to execute a *boca de calça*.

SAÍDA PARA O JOGO

The entrance of the player into the *roda* from the foot of the *berimbau* and the *reverencia*—both of which were briefly described previously—are also part of the *Angola* vocabulary, and show the subtleties and the sophistication of the player.

VOLTA DO MUNDO

It is not unusual for one of the players to suddenly interrupt the game and to start walking or jogging around the *roda*. The other accompanies him in the *volta ao mundo* without knowing what will come next—perhaps a sudden kick, or an invitation to return to the foot of the *berimbau* and start the game anew.

QUEDA DE RINS

Literally, kidney *(rin)* fall *(queda),* so named because in this movement the capoeirista's weight is balanced on his elbow, which in turn is placed near the kidney area. Both arms serve as support while the legs hang outstretched in the air.

In the drawing, one of the players in the *queda de rins* invites the other to jump through his outstretched legs.

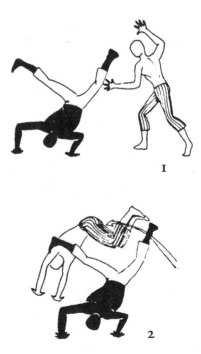

In short, *Capoeira Angola* is very rich in the kind of situations we have just described, in which both players are brought together to interact in ritualized ways. In the sequel to this book we intend to go into further detail on the subject matter.

FINAL WORDS

We have arrived at the end of our introductory exploration. The reader would do well to remember that the reality of the game is not simply the sum of the kicks, training methods and sequences shown here. Within the game, a player creates unique situations in which it is possible to release this or that kick or to proceed in this or that manner.

As your game develops further you will become aware that capoeira is not based on attack, but rather on *esquivas,* coming in under a kick and counterattacking or taking down the opponent.

Later—years later—the capoeirista gets the urge to enrich his or her game with aspects that have nothing to do with techniques or kicks but rather with the ritual of the game. There comes the urge to learn the aspects of *Angola* that we have just finished exploring. If this does not happen, the player can paint himself into a corner, and the game of capoeira can turn into a physical dispute, dull and frustrating.

We would hope that the final objective of showing the above kicks and exercises wouldn't be to have them repeated mechanically as illustrated in this book. The final objective is to prepare the capoeirista to react to diverse circumstances, improvising according to the situation and the moment at hand and, in a wider sense, learning how to look and interact in life in a way suggested by capoeira.

The philosophy and roots of capoeira come from the experience and knowledge of generations of players—how they played in the *roda* and how they played the game of life. The many kicks in this book are actually the result of improvisations that were successful in the past, and consequently became widely used, leading in time to the perfection of the movements, until they finally became considered traditional, classical kicks.

The moves and kicks shown here are like the letters of the alphabet: The exercises will teach the beginner to read and write. I hope that the reader eventually writes his or her own story, and plays the game in his or her very own way.

Nestor Capoeira

FINAL WORDS
TO THE ENGLISH EDITION

Since I first started teaching capoeira abroad in 1971 and, later on, when this *Little Book* was published in Brazil, I have always looked forward to an English version of my books.

But this is not easy. Capoeira is only beginning to spread its wings outside of Brazil, and few people have the insight to recognize that it is something that will become popular throughout the world in the next ten or twenty years. This means that, for the time being, publishing a book on capoeira is not attractive if you are looking for an immediate monetary return on your investment.

At the same time, I was afraid that the translation of the book would take away the flavor of its original version. Although I have lived for two years in the United States and five in Europe, I did not feel that my English was up to the task. I was lucky to meet Alex Ladd, who not only translated the book but also pinpointed special angles that would have to be further developed so that a reader from another culture could grasp meanings that are specific to Brazil.

I am very pleased with this final version. I hope that through it our *camaradas* from North America, England and other English-speaking countries will be able to share in the knowledge that has been passed down to us through generations of capoeira players.

Nestor Capoeira
Odenese, Denmark
November, 1994

GLOSSARY OF BASIC CAPOEIRA TERMS

(Compiled by A. Ladd)

Angola: *(See capoeira Angola)*

Arame: Literally 'wire.' An *arame* is attached to both extremeties of the *verga* (wooden bow) to create the berimbau. The *arame* is usually extracted from inside the inner rim of an old tire. Previously, animal entrails were used.

Atabaque: The drum used in capoeira *rodas*. Similar to the conga drum.

Baqueta: A wooden stick approximately 12 inches long used to strike the berimbau wire and thus create sound.

Berimbau: A bow-like percussive instrument which dictates the tempo of the music and consequently the tempo of the capoeira game. Commonly three types of berimbaus are present in the roda, the *gunga*, the *medio* and the *viola* or *violinha* (see those entries for more information). Mestre Bimba, however, opted for only one berimbau in the roda.

Cabaça: A gourd. To form the berimbau, the *cabaça* is dried out and hollowed. The *cabaça* is attached to the *verga* (wooden bow) and *arame* (wire) by way of a string ring to form a berimbau. The *cabaça* is the pecussive box which resonates the sound caused by striking the *arame* with the *baqueta* (small stick).

Capoeira Angola: With the advent of Mestre Bimba's *capoeira Regional* in the 1930s, the traditional capoeira became known as *capoeira Angola*. Generally performed to a slower rhythm, and movements are closer to the ground than in *Regional*. Games usually last longer and a premium is placed on the bodily dialog, the aesthetic qualities of the game and the *malandragem* (see entry for more information).

Capoeira Regional: A capoeira style created in Bahia in the1930s by Mestre Bimba (Manoel dos Reis Machado). Bimba modified many of the existing kicks in the traditional capoeira to create a more upright and aggressive style. *Regional* is usually practiced to a much quicker beat than Angola, usually to one of the several berimbau rhythms created by Bimba. Today the *Regional* style originally practiced by Bimba and his pupils is rarely seen. Instead there is a hybrid that could be called *Regional/Senzala* (see *Senzala* for more information).

Chulas: Can be used to denote chants in general, or a medium length chant, shorter than a *ladainha* but longer than a *corrido*.

Cintura desprezada: Literally 'scorned hips.' A sequence of four acrobatic exercises created by Mestre Bimba wherein the capoeirista learns to always fall on his feet.

Corpo fechado: Literally 'closed body.' A person who, through specific magic rituals, supposedly attains almost complete invulnerability in the face of various weapons.

Corridos: One or two verse songs sung by the "soloist" and answered by the chorus. The shortest among the three most common types of songs in the capoeira roda. *Corridos* are common in both capoeira *Angola* and *Regional.* The other two are the *ladainha* and the *quadras* (see those entries for more information).

Fundamentos: Literally 'basis' or 'origins.' Used to describe the philosophical roots of capoeira.

Gunga: The bass berimbau. When played in unison with the berimbau *medio* and the *violinha,* it is responsible for keeping the rhythm.

It normally plays the basic theme of a certain beat with very little variation. A particularly deep sounding *gunga* is also referred to as a *berra boi* ('bellowing ox' in Portuguese).

Jogo: Literally 'game' in Portuguese. Used to denote the activity inside the roda (circle). The verb is to *jogar* capoeira, i.e. to play capoeira.

Ladainha: The soulful songs that typically mark the begining of a roda or a game. The *ladainhas* are not call and response but rather are sung by a soloist, usually crouched at the foot of the berimbau. However, at the end of the *ladainha* the singer will go into a *canto de entrada,* where he praises capoeira mestres, places, or famous capoeiristas, and then the chorus responds in acknowledgement by repeating what was just praised. For example, the soloist will sing *Yê, viva Pastinha (Yê,* long live Pastinha). The chorus will then respond *Ê, viva Pastinha, camará.*

The *ladainhas* are typical of capoeira Angola. Mestre Bimba would not sing *ladainhas* in his rodas. instead he would sing *quadras* and *corridos* (see those entries for more information).

Malandro: A rogue or hustler. The *malandro* is a fixture in capoeira lore and in Brazilian popular culture in general. *Malandragem* is a tricky or deceitful act.

Mandinga: Magic or sorcery. The word implies a basic understanding of the forces of nature, and that the person in question knows how to use them by means of rituals involving magic. A *mandingueiro* is one well versed in *mandinga.*

Medio: Also known simply as berimbau or *berimbau de centro.* It plays the role similar to the rhythm guitar when played together with the *gunga* and the *violinha.* It typically plays the basic theme of a certain beat, then a basic variation on that theme, then it returns to the basic theme and so on.

Mestre: A capoeira master. Nowadays, many schools grant that title to students who have completed certain requirements. Traditionally, however, the title is conferred by capoeiristas themselves and the public at large to those who have proven themselves over many years (usually no less than ten) as both capoeiristas and teachers.

Pandeiro: The Brazilian tambourine.

Passo-à-dois: Literally, 'stepping in unison' in Portuguese. A ritualized movement typical of capoeira Angola. The *passo-à-dois* is initiated by one of the players inside the capoeira *roda* by stopping suddenly in the middle of a game and raising one arm or both arms. The other player then has to come and meet him in one of several prescribed manners, then together they take three steps forward, then three steps backwards and then cautiously resume the game.

Patúa: A magic amulet usually worn around the neck as protection against evil and injury.

Quadras: Four verse songs sung by the "soloist" and answered by the chorus. Typical of Mestre Bimba and capoeira *Regional.*

Rasteira: A sweep. One of the trademark capoeira moves.

Regional: *(see capoeira Regional)*

Roda: Literally means 'wheel' in Portuguese. This is the circle in which capoeira takes place. The roda is usually made up of other capoeiristas or bystanders standing or sitting in a circle.

Senzala: A capoeira group formed in Rio de Janeiro in the mid 1960s by a group of young capoeiristas. The Senzala group was responsible for adding several new warm up and teaching techniques. They also built on the work of Manoel dos Reis Machado (Mestre Bimba) and modified existing kicks and movements.

Verga: A stick usually about four to five feet tall which is used to form the berimbau bow. The *verga* is usually made from a Brazilian wood known as *biriba*. *Vergas* can also be made of other flexible woods or bamboo. A wire (usually removed from the inside rim of a tire) is attached to both extremities and a gourd (*cabaça*) is attached to the bottom to serve as a resonating box.

Vintém: An old coin used in Brazil and Portugal. Also used to denote the object used by the berimbau player to evoke different sounds from the berimbau. A *vintém* can be a heavy coin, a washer or a stone. By pressing the *vintém* hard against the *arame* (wire), you can produce a higher note, and by simply resting it against the wire you create a muffled sound. Not using the *vintém* at all produces the low note. The *vintém* can also be called a *dobrão*.

Viola (violinha): The berimbau that has the highest pitch; it has the most freedom to syncopate or to improvise when combined with other berimbaus (the *gunga* and the *medio*). The role that it plays is equivalent to that of the solos of a lead guitar.

For more information regarding capoeira groups in your area
contact:

The Capoeira Foundation
Jelon Vieira (Mestre Jelon)
105 Franklin St.,
New York, New York
10013
(212) 274-9737

Capoeira Bahia
Bira Almeida (Mestre Acordeon)
505 42nd Street
Richmond, California 94805
(510)236-8901